MOVING
MOUNTAINS

LESSONS on LIFE
and LEADERSHIP

REINHOLD
MESSNER

Executive
Excellence
Publishing

For permissions requests, contact the publisher at:

Executive Excellence Publishing
1366 East 1120 South
Provo, UT 84606
phone: 1-801-375-4060
toll free: 1-800-304-9782
fax: 1-801-377-5960
www.eep.com

For Executive Excellence books, magazines and other products, contact Executive Excellence directly. Call 1-800-304-9782, fax 1-801-377-5960, or visit our Web site at www.eep.com.

Printed in the United States

Based on the original German edition entitled:
Berg Versetzen: das Credo eines Grenzgängers
© BLV Verlagsgesellschaft mbH, München/Germany 1996

All photos courtesy of Reinhold Messner

Printed by Publishers Press

10 9 8 7 6 5 4 3 2 1

Library of Congress Cataloging-in-Publication Data

Messner, Reinhold, 1944-
    Moving mountains : lessons on life and leadership / Reinhold Messner.
        p. cm.
    ISBN 1-890009-90-3 (hardcover)
    1. Success—Psychological aspects. 2. Success in business. 3. Leadership. I. Title.

BF637.S8 .M46 2001
158—dc21
                                                                    00-067765

ADVANCE PRAISE
For *Moving Mountains*

"Forget 'how to' books on success and achievement. Messner shows that true success comes from winning on nature's terms through a clear understanding and personal conviction to the 'why' and 'what' that shape our dreams. *Moving Mountains* should be required reading for those committed to excellence and achievement."

—Sir Chris Bonington, Everest mountaineer, author, and lecturer

"Reinhold Messner is arguably the most gifted and visionary mountaineer of all time and one of the world's greatest athletes. He is also a highly respected professional. Living by his convictions, Messner has reached the pinnacle of success. He is extremely qualified to lend insight not only to those seeking to attain professional goals, but also to those seeking to live life as it should be lived—to satisfy their own souls.

This book has something for everyone. In its pages are many vibrant messages from the man who has learned so many vital lessons of life and business. Messner drives himself hard to satisfy his personal goals and aspirations, but also to enjoy inner peace. This book will help you find the free spirit that lies within you both personally and professionally."

—Ed Viesturs, climber of 12 8,000-ers without bottled oxygen

"If you ever wondered what inspired the world's most successful mountaineer along his arduous journey into the Himalayan Peaks above 8,000 meters and the Earth's great desert and polar regions, and, more importantly, how that might apply to your life and career, don't miss this book! Commingled with Messner's often complex and abstract philosophy are concrete interpretations and suggestions at the conclusion of each chapter. Messner's achievements riveted the mountaineering world and changed everyone's thinking on climbing style. Yet what emerges from this book that is, ultimately, philanthropic and timeless, is the portrait of an exceptional and compassionate human being who has enjoyed not only great success but also survived profound tragedy. Pick this book up and discover Messner's commitment to his own unique code of ethics and how his ideas apply across the universe of human endeavor."

—**Peter Athans, climber on 13 Everest expeditions, record for most Everest summits for a non-Sherpa**

"Messner is one of an elite group of individuals who have raised the bar of human achievement. I admire his determination, perseverance, and mental toughness which are all indispensable yet rare qualities necessary to attain the goals he achieved. *Moving Mountains* is a must-read for those whose aspirations extend beyond their current realities."

—**Karl Heinz Salzburger, President and CEO of The North Face**

"By being progressive, even aggressive, in his climbing career, Messner has accomplished the impossible. *Moving Mountains* outlines a simple course to success—in any field. This book will help you achieve your potential."

—**Lou Tice, President of The Pacific Institute and author of *Smart Talk***

CONTENTS

A Pearl of Great Price

by Ken Shelton

In creating this book of *Lessons on Life and Leadership*, I have been mesmerized by Reinhold Messner's strong personality and point of view. Like most genuine leaders, he transcends his field (mountain climber and expedition leader) and assumes a larger-than-life public image and persona. Privately, he remains a craftsman first, but his feats and his fame have also made him a spokesman. And in both arenas, he is a proven winner.

In business, attests Michael Eisner, CEO of Walt Disney Company, "the person with the strongest point of view usually wins the day."

Messner proves the point. Since meeting him at the International Book Fair in Frankfurt, Germany in 1999, I have been intrigued by his sagacity. It is one thing to have survived a few near-death experiences on mountains and in deserts and ice fields, but it is quite another to have learned so much and shared so deeply with the intent to benefit other people.

In creating this book, I have tried to be true to Messner in translation and intention. In recasting his ideas in a new context, some value is undoubtedly lost; hopefully, however, even more value is added in the process.

To assist you, the reader, in knowing and appreciating the man, Reinhold Messner, I have included a few of the tributes written by his colleagues; to assist you in reading with a sense of continuity, I have added section and chapter introductions; and to assist you in the assimilation and application of his ideas, I have added action items. Clearly, my intent is to make this book a powerful tool for personal, team, and organizational development.

I thank my son, Andrew Shelton, for bringing this project to us. I thank the German publishers, BLV, for their trust in our editing, for their faith in this project, and for their cordial and professional transfer of rights and photographs. I thank Doug Hagler and our translation team at Arthur International, our production designer Heidi Lawson, and our printer, Publishers Press.

If we have done our jobs well, you will be the big winner for making a wise investment of money, time, and effort in purchasing, reading, and acting on these powerful lessons—many of them coming to us at great price, one gratefully paid in the currency of persistence and pain by the author, legendary mountaineer and leader, Reinhold Messner.

Man, Myth, and Metaphor

by Herbert A. Henzler

As a myth, the mountain has moved entire nations and many generations of people. And mountaineering continues to have significant relevance for business management.

Several semantic parallels spring into mind: the career climb, peak performance, the rope-team as an expression of team leadership, the Sherpas as indispensable helpers in great ventures, and all elements of teamwork, risk management, and creative expression.

The lectures and books by Reinhold Messner correlate the experience of extreme mountain climbing with excellent management. From Messner's grandiose visions and expeditions—such as his solo ascent of Mount Everest without an oxygen mask, the crossing of the Antarctic without technological support, the climbing of all 14 of the 8,000-meter mountains in the world, and the lengthwise crossing of the Takla Makan—we can easily imagine how such visionary quality could offer rich inspiration for new automobiles, aircraft, communication systems, buildings, and e-business. Arising automatically from his mind are ideas connected to all the revolutionary management concepts, such as "just in time" logistics, "speed to market," "reengineering," "innovation," "globalization," "diversity," "teamwork," and "leadership."

Reinhold Messner, born in 1944, was 20 years old in 1964 when the last 8,000-meter mountain was climbed. He arrived on the scene too late to make a first ascent of any of the 14. However, his climb of Hidden Peak in 1975 was only the second time the summit had been reached. He climbed two other 8,000ers as third ascents, two as fourth, one as fifth. All his climbs of 8,000-meter peaks fall into the first 20 successful ascents. No one else will ever be able to match such a low count. It was in 1982 that Reinhold Messner consciously resolved to climb all of the 8,000ers. A strong desire for extreme experience was the motivating force.

Messner's innovative strategy and efficient logistics allowed him to succeed with a minimum of support from human resources and high technology. On Messner's fast and flexible treks, no oxygen bottles, no provisions, and no accommodating tents for troops of helpers needed to be carried up the mountain. We hear on occasion of Messner breaking off expeditions, but these "failed" expeditions placed him in the position to master other demanding projects carried out at a later date. Almost every entrepreneur can remember their own development projects: some that got stuck in a pointless loss of time, and others that should have been discontinued so that time, energy, and resources could be used elsewhere to meet cost and quality demands.

We see conscious phases of progress in Reinhold Messner's life and career—from a solo climber, to a mountaineer in the Himalayas, to an expedition leader, to a crosser of deserts and ice fields. In the spirit of Daniel Levinson, these "Seasons of Man's Life" have inspired him to new and greater heights, and to make other phases of his life possible. His concentration on the essential, his bias for action, his respect for people, his love of life, and his care for the environment and are among the secrets of success that the best managers share with Reinhold Messner. They are not stuck to their chairs; they do not miss the appropriate time for bailing out; and they certainly don't waste time in looking for ways to record their deeds for posterity.

Messner has repeatedly renounced becoming a film maker and actor. He has, on the one hand, "remained true to his talent"—perfecting it over the course of many years and developing it continuously. On the other hand, the Messner of year 2000 has much in common with the Messner of 1970 in the determination and independence in pursuing goals, but he is a different man today—a better and wiser man. In earlier days, the solo mountaineering performance excited him. Today, he is more philosophical and contemplative about mountain climbing. Where once a tremendous sense of adventure motivated him, it is now the problem of ecological imbalance and the search for a solution.

I know a number of business people who undertake long hikes to become open for new ideas. Only those who do what gives them pleasure in their lives, what they do with enthusiasm, what they do wholeheartedly, will be successful.

The idea for a book of Reinhold Messner's insights on life and leadership came about during our conversations on a tour of South America and the inevitable waiting for suitable weather to climb the Chimborazo. Over the years, Messner has repeatedly impressed me with his easy access to the challenges of people and project management, and with his insights and personal experiences related to personal, team, and organizational leadership. These ideas became intensified as he worked on this book. I am certain that his insights will serve as valuable instruments for contemplation and motivation—not only for every business manager, but also for every person who aspires to climb or move whatever mountain stands in the way of personal fulfillment and professional success.   **MM**

Awakening Dreams and Hopes

by Takashi Osaki, climber of six 8,000ers

A lot of people, including himself, believed that Reinhold Messner would eventually climb all 14 of the 8,000-meter mountains—that his success hung in the air. All the same, as an Alpinist who has been much influenced by Messner, I was delighted when he pulled it off.

As I try and follow his example, the scale of his achievement is clear. Climbing a summit of over 8,000 meters in a small group or alone, without oxygen equipment, in Alpine style, by difficult routes—these "Messnerish conditions" form the basis of top climbing activity today. His attempt to push our mental and physical limits in increasingly adventurous "games," without being dependent on artificial aid in the way of apparatus or equipment, has become a new mountaineering philosophy.

When Messner appeared in the world of Himalayan Alpinists, such thoughts were rare. He only felt challenged on the summits of the world, and not by mountains. His methods, full of romanticism and new ideas, were unthinkable before then. He discovered and demonstrated them. His record is therefore exceedingly impressive and fascinating. It is as if he alone constituted the whole history of modern mountaineering.

Messner was the first to practice systematic training for his activity in the Himalaya: exercises to rob you of breath in preparation for climbing under extreme conditions and on high summits. He has achieved a mental and physical toughness and an endurance that is unique.

Climbing all 14 of the 8,000ers is an unbelievable feat. It must have been a hard road for Messner. His 29 expeditions to 8,000ers in 16 years tell little of the immeasurable energy necessary to keep a firm grip on the resolution, of the overcoming of self-doubt, and of his many setbacks. Above everything they demonstrate his total harmony of body and mind, the bedrock upon which his philosophy is founded.

Climbing at top level, in the demanding conditions of extreme altitude, certain death can be expected from even the slightest error. Whether an Alpinist can come through such demands unscathed or not depends upon his self-regulating facility. That means, whether he has or has not the instinctive, practical, and intellectual capability to distill life from death. Messner "climbed over the dangers" that came at him thick and fast. That was, and is, his art—an art nourished by judgment sharp enough to evaluate dangerous situations precisely, and a relish in decision-making. He has earned the skill to do this from his numerous high-altitude experiences. Real adventure (which does not exist without extreme danger) and survival are two opposing problems. Messner has established that you can come back alive—even out of hell.

On those expeditions where Messner has met with no climbing success, I have been amazed by his clear and humble attitude. If the danger is incalculable, he turns his back on it, time and again. Messner faces the unknown with the strength of an innocent and childlike heart. He has tried to discover this within himself, and in so doing has furthered his own potential.

By uncovering many wonderful "play opportunities" with his own hands, feet and heart, he has furnished proof of a whole new secret world within ourselves. All 14 of the 8,000ers, the record itself, which he has gained, is important. But what he has done that is more important is that he has awakened dreams and hopes and the spirit of adventure in people throughout the world. **MM**

A Shining Star

*by Mathias Rebitsch, member of the
1938 expedition to Nanga Parbat*

A climbing star has been shining for decades, attracting increasing attention. The "Reinhold" is now a standard (like the gold standard). His rock climbs were ever more audacious. He climbed the hardest routes solo; put up new direct routes of the most extreme difficulty, on the smoothest of walls, at the very top end of the range; and joined other climbers in making first winter ascents of Grade Six faces.

His exploits have surpassed all previous achievement. He has undercut all normal climbing times. He has complete mastery of free-climbing times and techniques. Calm in the face of danger, foresighted planning, and deliberate execution mark him. For Reinhold Messner, rock would appear to present no further problems. A climbing genius—or perhaps only a rock acrobat?

Messner came to the Western Alps, and there, too, he stood everything on its head with the swiftest ascent times. In so doing, he demonstrated that he is as much at home on steep ice and mixed ground as on rock. His toughness and driving force are exceptional, as are his almost inexhaustible reserves of strength.

Messner had yet to demonstrate his worth on expeditions to the world's big mountains. This he did in 1970, when he climbed the Rupal face of Nanga Parbat!

Reinhold Messner has burst through the existing limits of Alpine knowledge and redefined standards. A towering phenomenon! And yet, he is by no means a robust, muscular woodcutter type; rather, he is sensitive, slim, fine-limbed, conditioned to the last fibre, and driven by inner fire, drawing the strength for his undertakings more from his psychological reserves.

The essential key to his almost unbelievable ability to pull off what he sets out to do, the way he copes with altitude, really lies in his systematic autogenous training, in the yoga type exercises he practices to maintain conscious control over his body. He shows rational expenditure of strength directed by sharp intellect.

The Rupal face of Nanga Parbat is the highest wall in the world—an unbelievably huge 4,500 meter-high buttress of snow and ice, the epitome of "unclimbability." The ascent of the Rupal face is the boldest climb ever done—and may well be the hardest on any 8,000-meter mountain. Having made a first ascent of its most difficult face, Reinhold and Gunther Messner came down on the other side of the mountain, down 3,500 meters of unknown ice and snow, into a strange, uninhabited glacier valley. They had to rely solely on their own resources; there was no chain of camps, nor could they expect any help from friends. A pioneering act such as this has never been seen in the history of the Himalayas!

Section I

*   *   *

My Search for Meaning and Happiness

In a sense, every quest—every attempt at pathbreaking and pioneering—is a search for meaning and fulfillment, often in response to a clarion call that comes in the form of a vision or dream. The response is fueled by a sense of adventure and ambition. And the result is an authentic happiness, an enduring joy, and a self-knowledge that timid souls will never know.

Reinhold Messner makes it very clear: he is first and foremost a dreamer, but one who keeps one foot in reality. As he says, in his business—and perhaps in any other—survival over time is far and away the most meaningful measure of success.

Chapter 1

Questions, Motives, Meaning

The basis for success on any mountain or in any field, writes Messner, is the inner process of spiritual creation—a process that may first require moving the mountains in our minds. It certainly requires addressing all the relevant "why" questions. Motives are always challenged. And when the nature of the business involves great risk and the outcome seen as "useless," the very mission is challenged. But in Messner's book, even "useless" activities can be very meaningful because we all have the right and responsibility to give meaning to events through the exercise of our faith and our actions.

✳ ✳ ✳

Spiritual Creation

Every adventure, quest, and border-crossing requires an inner process of spiritual creation. At least for me. And this spiritual creation is—as in any artistic or industrial enterprise—the basis for later success. Anyone who wants to change something first must change his point of view and his position, then the positions of his coworkers. In life, it is more important to move the mountains in our minds than simply to plant a tree or to leave a footprint.

Why Not Stay Below?

On the way back down a mountain, I sometimes ask myself, "Why don't I stay below?" "Why don't I just stay home and become a hermit?" "Why not take up my quarters in some secluded district for the rest of my life?" But I know that I could not do it. I am inwardly just as dependent on civilization as on my expeditions. One reason I need these expeditions is because I have a terrible fear of otherwise wasting away my life. I want my life to mean something.

Questions of Life

This state of merging into infinity is a sensation I have frequently experienced on big mountains, and it always seems to accentuate the existential questions of our existence: Why are we here? Where do we come from? Where are we going? Personally I have not discovered any definite answers. And, if you discount religion, there are no answers. The state of being active within life activates the fundamental questions of life. But when I am up on a mountain, I rarely question what I am doing or why I am there. The climbing, the concentration, the struggle to push myself forward—those are the answers—because those are the basic purposes of life. In effect, I become my own answer: the questions all cancel out.

Self-Discovery

My expeditions have enabled me to draw closer to myself, to see into myself more clearly. The higher I climb, the deeper I see within myself. But if I were to put all sorts of technical gadgets between myself and the mountain, I would miss certain experiences and feelings and insights. If, for example, I were to wear an oxygen mask, I wouldn't know exactly what it means to climb at heights of 8,000 meters or more, what it feels to struggle against the body's resistance. If I had never done solo climbs, I would not know what it feels like to endure the loneliness of being totally beyond the reach of help of another person. I see the usefulness of climbing not so much in the further development of technique, rather in the development of our instincts and our abilities to extend ourselves. Learning about our limitations is just as important as our claim to be able to do anything—with the knowledge that God is the ultimate solution.

Trial of Faith

Some days climbing is so easy. On other days each step is an ordeal. My progress is slow or stopped. The rucksack weighs more heavily. On those days, I feel lost and vulnerable. So it is with faith and belief. On some days, I cannot make myself believe that there is a God who governs this world, who concerns himself with each single one of us. I prefer to believe that there is no creator outside of me, outside of the cosmos. I don't know when this faith was lost to me; I only know that since losing it, it is more difficult not to feel myself alone and forsaken in this world. At last I must accept being alone, inevitably alone. This is not to say that I am not a spiritual person. The spiritual, finely-tuned person is unlimited, and this person's experience possibilities are unlimited. His or her potential is unlimited. My potential is only realized when I physically transpose spiritual possibilities, when I realize spiritual experiences and spiritualize physical experiences.

Look to the Mountains for Answers

If I do not give you enough answers in this book, don't come looking to me for more—go to the mountains! We humans give too many answers to each other. The mountains have an answer for everyone—and each day there are new answers.

My Motives

What is my motive for climbing mountains? For my own part, I do not come to Everest or any other mountain because I have an ambition to climb it at any price. My primary desire is to get to know it, in all its magnitude, its difficulty and harshness. I am determined to forego the summit if I can't reach it unaided by breathing equipment. Modern oxygen apparatus has the effect of reducing the height of Everest to about 6,000 meters. If I want this experience, I don't have to go to Everest at all. But if I want to experience Everest's unique sheer bulk, then to be able to feel it and sense it, I have to climb without any technical tricks. Only then will I know what a man feels like being there, what new dimensions it opens up for him, and whether he can thereby learn anything new in terms of his relationship with the cosmos.

Why Risk?

Now more than ever, the whys and wherefores of any risky adventure or enterprise are discussed and debated in public. "What is the sense in attempting to climb Mount Everest?" people ask me. "Such attempts cost not only human lives, privations and sorrow, but also a great deal of money, and yet the usefulness is practically nil." In response, climbers try to clarify what it means to them. The most obvious good is an increased knowledge of our own capacities. By trying with all our might and with all our mind, we are getting to know better what we can do. No one can say for certain whether we can or cannot reach the summit.

My Creed

The passionate creed of all adventurers regarding life is the expression of desire, which, increased by fear, is perceived as a fullness of meaning with no further inquiry. Whether this spontaneous experience of sense only leads to a short-term artificial sense of meaning or whether the intellectual problem of meaning pales instead, I do not know. I know, however, that I don't ask during or after strong experiences what I am living for. It is as if I can feel meaning in my body, as if I can catch sight of it in the wilderness like a clear thought. The adventurer does not turn the world on its head, but that person who affirms all around with everything that is dear and precious to him or her. With this type of meaningful experience we can find meaning and give meaning, when we have weighed it all. Every one of us can. When I find something— a deed, thing, person, or idea—important, beautiful, or fascinating, I make it, he, or she meaningful. We not only have the right, but also the duty, to give meaning. In a sense, meaning can not be found, and so it does not need to be sought. It also does not come alone and is not expected. Meaning is given and made by us.

Useless but Meaningful

I emphasize that "meaningful" is not interchangeable with "useful." I stand by the statement that my activity is useless. But it can still be meaningful, depending on my frame of mind, from my identity, and from my unity with my actions. I have never understood why so many people become slaves to so many sects, why they search for their living standards in religions, why they hunger for definite points of meaning. To allow others to give you meaning makes you blind. I do not contend that religions are wrong. Religious teachings have been of great importance for many groups of people for centuries. But I wish to grasp meaning in myself.

The useless activity of climbing mountains can be very meaningful. Often when I am en route—not only in difficult, critical moments but also on early mornings at sunrise or at the return from life-threatening surroundings to flowing water and flowers—there are no questions to be asked. Because I am the answer myself. All doubts are lifted through my being, through my actions, through this, my return. The meaning in me is defined through what I do, even when others consider my activity to be useless.

The Meaning of Life

The meaning of my life no longer lies simply in my head during passages in the frontier. It can be intuitively felt. In the subconsciousness, the outer- and inner-worlds are vitally linked. This leads a person to a native understanding of his oneness with the cosmos. Is this unity only possible through adventure? In such moments, at least, the I becomes Self, and death is no longer the horrible end. Afterwards death is still death, but with other meaning.

The more I become convinced that adventures are the "conquest of the useless," the more I doubt the usefulness of all human deeds. In the end, what benefits, as well as injuries, are brought to society and to the cosmos? Meaning is more important than benefits.

In the novel *Discovery of Slowness,* author Sten Nadolny finds meaning in deeds which are set outside of all reason, which apparently dispense with every rational sense. Even though the story finally ends with the survival of the main character, the meaning of life does not lie simply in preservation: "Abilities that are not employed do not exist." In this context, one can not ask questions of "survival of the fittest." Our spirits reach far beyond the purely practical question of survival toward the transcendent meaning in life.

The Creation of Meaning

I have been saved from barely survivable situations not only once but several times by hallucinations. Even though I played with hope, for which there was no justification, I never felt like a fool afterwards.

I know today that we are not indestructible somethings, but we are a process, a variable state of progression. Because of this I have just as little fear of life as I do of death, and I wish no limits. I cannot think of anything I have not experienced. Mountain climbing for me is not primarily a flight from the intolerable conditions of western society; mountain climbing for me is creation of meaning. Why does any man or woman willingly go into the fringe areas of mortal survival possibilities, on the edges of his or her capacity, when he or she has more than the basic necessities of life? Much for the same reasons that someone searches for achievement: because of ambition, vanity, desire. When the basic necessities of life are satisfied, time and strength are left for us to play with, and our energies, our ideas, our abilities need to be played out. For this we harvest a feeling of self-worth, love of life and, above all, meaning.

We Give Meaning to Life

Meaning is not established for us from the outside. We give meaning to life. I leave open the question about God. But the question about meaning is not only a matter of religion. I know that for hundreds of years, religion was exclusively recognized to establish meaning. But I also know that we can establish meaning ourselves. How much easier life would be if there were an "eternal meaning" and a "unmoving order." If only I did not have to always newly discover these. To establish meaning is half the effort in life, and it also is the most risky. Just the passage to the cosmos is enough for me to comprehend myself as a part of it. In the chaos that we never completely see through, and in the apparent order, which we believe to know according to natural law, is meaning not given, but afterwards it is interpretable.

My Life, My Meaning

I do not think much of our "I'm okay, you're okay" society that pushes death away and mutually tells lies out of a desire for life, optimism, and health—as if sickness were sin, fear laughable, and confidence an obligation. But I, too, belong to this society, whether I wish to or not. Since my "death experience" at Nanga Parbat, I have had much more courage than earlier to stand up to my life, to my fears, to my meaning. It is not that I have been freed from all fears of death, but the truth became clear that nothing and no one besides me personally gives me life meaning. I try to live my life with an over-exposed individual consciousness and thereby attempt to destroy no one else's. So I am well-balanced, satisfied, full of peace. According to my experience, people become unsatisfied and aggressive when they are not allowed to live their lives; when they suppress their feelings, their fears, their dreams; when they receive the purpose and meaning of their lives from outside themselves.

Who Are the Founders of Meaning?

I am not suggesting that my meaning justifies everything. Today we live too much on a limited earth. I am astonished with how perfect our suppressive mechanics function against the great dangers—the global ecological dangers (reduction of the ozone layer, reactor accidents, rapid climate changes) and the social dangers (overpopulation in Asia and Africa, massive human migration). It is as if an entire appeasement industry is engaged to push away fears and facts in this context. Except for a few environmentalists and scientists, only children ask today with fear, "Can the Earth still be saved?" Where are the founders of meaning who are capable of tackling the tough ecological and social questions? When life or death situations arise, fear begins—as does the question of meaning. My repeated adventures have much to do with a desire for fear, knowing that between desire and fear, meaning is found.

Quality of Life

The progressive alienation of mankind from nature becomes more clear when I am underway in the wilderness or on a mountain. Perceptions emerge suddenly like pictures from nothingness. Often feelings become knowledge, without going through the thought process. It's as if the unconscious mind up there at an awake state becomes even more awake. It is like a trance or a peaceful sleep. It propagates positive thoughts and harmonious feelings. This state defines quality of life for me, not a second vehicle or a VCR.

Add Meaning to Deeds

Never have I consciously put more meaning in my activities, but meaning was an obvious assumption for my successes. Naturally I wish to also express with my deeds, and I also must always create. But both these necessities would not have allowed me to go as far as I always have tried. The meaning, which my adventures have, carries me and my world. I believe that it is possible to achieve a goal with meaning. However, no one is immune to doubt, including me. I often place my deeds in question. Sporadic, before I set out. Fatigue, life-threatening situations, and burnout can be the release. But doubt normally does not last long. At least when beginning an expedition, during the journey I am completely lost with the moment. As if there were nothing more meaningful on this earth. Nevertheless, there is no better and no worse meaning. He who is more capable of putting more meaning in his deeds will be more successful.

Counterfeit Character

I have often been able to expose people who continually speak of ideals in this context as pretentious thinkers. They conceal with their moral code, with the banner of idealism that they carry before them, the demands they place on others without restraint. The tasks they take on are not important to them; the demands they raise are. In the end, it reflects their character. I have the latent dissatisfaction that is found with a large part of the modern meritocracy—especially that which is found with those who praise idealism, altruism, and subordination of desire as their virtues. They are determined to be different. Their idealism rises from a hunger for recognition. Their altruism is an excuse. Their subordination is a hiding game. They fundamentally reject placing individual demands on themselves, discovering challenges for themselves.

Feigned Idealism

Idealism usually arises from a concept determined from the outside. To be an idea creator, meaning giver, law giver, and decision maker is not a privilege, but a requirement for a border crosser. All "selfless" border-crossers are suspect to me. They have no goals except those that seem somewhat "special." My experiences give me the right to expose them as parasites. They "live" on feigned idealism and mostly from direct or indirect criticisms by their "colleagues," through which they pretend to rise up. I am always a doer.

What Meaning Does Life Have?

Anyone who does nothing else throughout his adult life, the whole day, every week, 11 months a year, other than work in order to provide for his wife and children and to be able to drink beer in the evening in front of the television, will ask himself continually, "Why am I sitting at this machine? What meaning does life have at all? Is this all there is?" It is completely different for the one who is able to express himself with his most primitive abilities. For him, the fatalistic question of the meaning of life is not asked; new strength flows constantly into him. Creative "flow" arises from his industry and integrity.

My Morality

I stand by the statement that my action is its own goal. Perhaps I am also a representative of all who would like to make my border crossings, but are handicapped because they do not have sufficient time, means, or ability to apply to doing it. But this is secondary. When I stand by my egotism, I am often like a condemned person who lives outside all ethics and morals. Here morals are only a measuring unit found in human beings in the behavior of people toward one another, who often exclude any claim to themselves. I believe that I can do anything I can and want as long as I disturb neither other people's spheres nor the balance of the Universe.

My egotism in this is not more reprehensible than that of a technician who constructs an automobile, an artist who paints a picture, or a doctor who wants to help his patients. Like anyone else, I am a part of a greater society, even though I go away from this society from time to time to be alone or in a small group to hike through the wilderness. My border-crossings have shown me that we humans are similar, act similarly, and think similarly. The fact that there are many others who are different is not evidence against our basic similarity. They are hiding behind a mask or a moral code and emphasize their ethical values unceasingly. This too is only human. No one can keep their mask on during a border crossing. The recognition process that triggers every trip does not concern me only; it also concerns the behavior and being of others. And while in the border field of psychophysics everyone takes off his mask, we experience many things above us. This is also all too human. And shouldn't this be beneficial? MM

*　*　*

Application and Action

Application: In your life and organization, do you go through the "spiritual creation" process at the outset of each quest? Do you envision in your mind the outcome? Do you ask yourself the tough "why" questions and examine your motives? Do you have a creed or mission statement? Do you consider how you might add more meaning to every activity in your life? Messner promises: "Those who put more meaning in their deeds will be more successful." Do you hold to your beliefs without false idealism, counterfeit character, or feigned optimism—hiding behind a mask as opposed to being open, honest, and authentic?

Action: Consider three ways to add more meaning to your life and work, knowing that from this meaning comes your motivation to achieve peak performance. **AA**

Chapter 2
Dreams and Visions

Like most great athletes, entertainers, business executives and entrepreneurs, Reinhold Messner is driven by dreams and guided by visions. These, much more than fame and fortune, supply the "inner momentum" needed to climb a mountain, overcome a barrier, or cross a border. By looking for the "possible in the impossible" and "reality in the romance," Messner manages not only to escape death but also to find life in the mountains. His dream of climbing Everest "by fair means" becomes the standard, and to reach it he must employ the practice of visualizing the performance in advance.

* * *

Inner Momentum

Not "where from" but "where to" carries me to the next mountain and beyond myself. I leave it to be seen how far an idea will be viewed as an inspiration, an act of will, or an invention. Once recognized as energy, a vision can be thought through further until it becomes a real utopia. A thought structure becomes supporting, so that the vision can be realized in the form of an action, a work of art, or an industrial product. Computers have little courage and are not suitable for border-crossings. Players who have "lost their head" interest me more. The growth of an idea into inner momentum leads, if it is strong enough, to a concept that presses formally to completion. The more harmonious a real utopia is, the clearer the concept is and the greater the chances for success are.

31

From Vision to Success

Success depends initially on the ability to develop strong visions, and then on being true to ourselves, on endurance, on the directness with which we convert our real utopias into actions. My border-crossings bring me back to my origin, because in that way I can be wholly myself. Out of this self-identification, I create new ideas, energy, and new strength. Between idea and action stretches identification, like the string between the two ends of a bow. I am not a computer, machine, or official. What have school and education made of me? Nothing! But I do not function like refrigerators and exemplary citizens do. I daydream first, then I am pregnant with an idea and go after a strong real utopia. The rest is commonplace, but often a fascinating commonplace.

A Dreamer First

The limit of what is possible can be reached only in small steps. The nearer I get to this limit, the smaller these steps have to be. Even with both feet on the ground, I am still a dreamer. I have never stopped developing realizable utopias, and I will only give up my "madness" when nothing more occurs to me. What others think about it remains very secondary. There is a challenge in doing something that has never been done before; even more, doing something even when all others have considered it impossible. This has nothing to do with seeking records. Even if I reach the limit of performance; that is not what I am looking for in my climbing and border crossings. Putting a real utopia into action involves much more. In crossing borders, I am first of all a dreamer or innovator, and second of all an implementer or developer.

Fantasy or Reality?

I look for the possible in the impossible—the reality in the daydream. Many people change their wishes into fantasy images, without ever realizing them. I aim as high (good, far, successful) as possible and then push the limits of human performance. For me a daydream is not a castle in the sky—it is fantasy plus knowledge. I challenge what others consider impossible. Visionary individuals and enterprises think ecologically, are future-related, and change something. People without vision are not innovators, only implementers and developers. They don't move mountains; some don't even leave footprints.

Visualizing the Dream

One of my daydreams was to climb the most difficult wall on the highest mountain in the world. The highest mountain in the world has a special attraction. I prepared myself for my solo climb of Everest like I hadn't trained for many years. In doing this, I never asked myself how hard I had to work to make a lot of money from any success or recognition I might obtain. For me, the daydream of "Everest by fair means" was an *idée fixe*. I identified myself with the standard, the summit of Everest, so that I looked up toward it during my training, when I woke up in the morning, and in so many dreams in a kind of advance visualization of the performance.

My Own Invention

Many people can climb Mount Everest with an oxygen mask, imbedded in the safety network of a large expedition. My dream was to climb the highest mountain in the world in Alpine style. This dream was a real utopia, but it allowed ambition to arise, as well as sensitivities (aesthetics, beauty of an action). "Everest by fair means"—it was like an invention that arose slowly and as a whole, intuitively. For me, this dream involves less the limits of human performance than the creation of possibility. I believe in my invention. I am living with it in spirit, so that in the end it is as if nothing else exists. The fact that all others consider my real utopias to be unrealizable and dangerous hardly disturbs me. It strengthens me in my awareness of risking something exceptional. It doesn't make me slow down.

Dreams Change Reality

Anyone who not only has or dreams ideas, but lets them grow, forms them into real utopias, and also brings strength, endurance, and stamina to convert them into action, always changes something. In contrast to those who are always satisfied with the status quo; even more so those who are committed to maintaining the status quo (out of fear or comfort, because they are familiar with the facts). Whoever risks realization of a real utopia risks failure. He learns that identification with the dream leads to dominance of the unusual over the usual and to commitment with respect to the dream.

Vision More than Genius

Success comes from enthusiasm and commitment. Intuition is less a part of it than generally assumed—genius even less. Intuition surely has an important place. But I consider visions as more important. Discipline and creativity are followed by a process of fermentation, and genius does not give that without diligence. Intuition can be analyzed. It is based on studies and experiences. It always comes down to how long I have lived with something.

Genius is as rare as heroism—and both ideas have likely been thought up by a few intellectuals to shine their own images. Only the sum of many experiences and knowledge gives intuition. Some people call this genius. Many outsiders explain my actions as "superhuman." This is a big mistake. I am a completely normal person. Most healthy people could also do what I do or have done. They would only have to want what I want—crossing Antarctica and climbing Mount Everest—with the same vehemence.

The Power of Faith

What happens before the event is as important as the event itself: the self-preparation, subjecting oneself to the task, being into the thing. The actual climbing of Mount Everest is only the last step. My last step depends on my first step, and my first step must depend on the last—for the idea is dependent on the initiative. This image is true for every action. Whether an idea can be implemented depends on some associated circumstances: the power of this idea, many important steps, primarily a belief in the goal. They do not depend only on the creator of the idea. How often are ideas constricted, minimized, and lost from view because they remain hanging in empty space! How much creative power is wasted because the ideas are not able to create faith!

Visions Have a Life of Their Own

I consider my visions more or less my own. They can grow and ripen only in the quiet. They only become daydreams if they are strong enough to develop into a life of their own as a real utopia. Thus it is not my image that lets me grow, but my ideas, my plans, my dreams, and my visions. Vision is a basic requirement of growth and progress. Vision and identification with the goal are what allow our motivation to grow over months to the energy of will that makes the body into an arrow. Only stored energy carries far. It explodes (or implodes) in action.

Vision as a Real Utopia

Every person has dreams. Sooner or later, he either seeks experiences for these dreams or he gives up and suppresses them. It is better to identify yourself with your dreams and live them out. I know that reality and daydream can become equivalent. With the evidence that even Mount Everest can be achieved without oxygen masks and artificial means and that all mountains can be climbed in the Alpine style, I postulated a valid game rule: Mountain climbs should also be environmentally friendly and elegant. Unfortunately, this statement went down, and it is not my style to preach.

To be possessed (by a vision, dream, or idea) means not being free. It is captivity. As an action man, I soon plan the next step: the realization of a new real utopia. Thus, as a visionary, I make out of the future a plan that can be experienced. The desire or ambition to climb as high as possible, as far as possible, is often understood as seeking records or recognition. That aim will not get you very far or very high.

Converting your dream into reality involves three steps: first, you think or dream something up—you have an idea or impression; next, you develop a real utopia in your head; and third, you convert that utopia into reality. This process not only leads to a heightened success experience but also a strong feeling of unity. Being one with spirit, body, and the universe is what border-crossing is all about.

All my actions have started with an idea in my head. But as long an idea is there only as a vague imagination, it has little power. Only when it grows like a child in its mother's body, when it solidifies into a realizable utopia, can it be born and must be realized. When I talk about daydreams, I don't mean castles in the sky. My daydreams are much more real. Naturally, a daydream has only sprung out of my fantasies. But my experience and my knowledge permit the conclusion—at least in theory—to convert it into action.

Follow Your Dreams

The only way discontent can be reduced, especially among the wealthy, is by the courage of people to follow their ideas. Each of us has individual abilities; each of us is pre-destined to accomplish certain achievements. We push ourselves because of this inclination. If only each person would allow himself or herself to go where their dreams are leading them! Sadly, only a few people are ready for the task. Life fears hinder many people from taking control of their own lives. Fate is too often described as a power from without that we cannot influence. I denote fate as our aptitude to be ourselves. You are your own fate. Your path corresponds to you. There are as many different paths as there are people. When young people ask me what they must do to become as successful an adventurer as they believe me to be, I dissuade them from following my path. My path cannot become their path; it can only help the search for theirs. My way was, or perhaps is (not always!) right for me. It is surely false for all others.

Composed of Dreams

I am composed of many dreams. Maybe this is why it is so easy for me to forget difficult and painful moments and to gain a new sense of adventure. My life before me thrills me and motivates me—not death, which I have left behind me so many times. At high altitudes I experience increasing dream activity. And during long expeditions, past experiences turn into feelings. It is as if my recollections are mixed anew. It is as if the man on foot—as a dream dancer who no longer judges his life with moral standards, but with aesthetic ones, one who believes in soaring—bridges the gap between thought and action. In doing so, he becomes completely present, a complete being with more clarity of thought and more self-awareness.

Fantasy Flight

Journeys into self-experience can distance you ever more from other people and lead to a sort of morbid preoccupation with fantasy. It hurts me that during my expeditions neither on the outward nor on the homeward journey do I take enough time for the people whom I meet. Something in me constantly makes me uneasy after a short time, as if I had a train to catch. It gives me no peace. Torn between flight and quest, I am condemned to climbing, and it does not surprise me that recently in one dream, I appeared as the Flying Dutchman, sailing across the unending sea of a shattered glacier in a ship of shredded canvas.

Life Calling or Mission

My main profession, adventuring, is not included in the standard list of careers because it brings in nothing. It is my calling. Just as animals and plants have missions, so has humankind a mission since the beginning. It is not as if I preach this standard of living as one who reached happiness by my own deeds. Just the opposite: I accept the schooling, the instruction, the specialization, but only as a necessary evil.

Driven by a Dream

I was always a dreamer, and am still a dreamer. Whenever an idea takes hold of me, it brings with it a spontaneous burst of strength, and this reaction has become stronger over the years. It is a feeling of relief that permeates me to the very tips of my toes; it is like a great weight being lifted from my chest, even knowing that I am committing myself into danger. With a new idea in my head, I become single-minded, guided by this idea, carried along, driven. There can be no more freedom then. People who say I planned my adventures for mercenary reasons have no conception of this inner explosion of the soul. Calculating people are usually faint-hearted, seldom capable of going to the limits. Gamblers who have lost their nerve interest me more. Man is not born as Ulysses; he allows himself to be tempted out of his everyday tracks by curiosity, even by ambition, but never by money, and still less by envy. MM

*　*　*

Application and Action

Application: What is the source of the motivation and direction in your personal life and in your profession? Messner states: "Success depends initially on the ability to develop strong visions." How might you develop strong visions and passionate dreams, knowing that "dreams change reality"? Do you employ the practice of visualization of your performance in advance? Do you follow your dreams, give flight to your fantasies, and realize your utopias?

Action: Much of Messner's life and writing serves as a primer in applied faith—how to make active the faith you have in yourself, your dreams, your goals, your God. Seek experiences for your dreams to convert your "utopias" into realities. **AA**

Chapter 3
Adventure, Action, and Ambition

Real adventure, suggests Messner, means seizing opportunities, testing our strengths against the unknown and discovering our own unique potential. Inevitably, it means leaving behind comfort zones and homes and "thinking with our legs." The "bias for action" is shared not only by most explorers but also by all who excel at their work. Better to make an ad hoc decision now than none at all. Better to act chaotically than do nothing in an orderly way. We come alive in adventure. Those who venture nothing gain nothing. Without healthy ambition, we may settle for a passive existence, feeling resigned to some fate. Positive ambition leads to a life of adventure.

✳　✳　✳

Real Adventure

I seldom use the word "adventure" anymore, because it has been worn out and emptied of all content. Everyone today can book a trip, tour, or vacation that is sold in the catalog as an "adventure." An organized adventure, however, is an oxymoron. Successful border-crossers are neither the best of the unshockable nor gifted fear-dispellers. They only learn that courage and fear are equally valuable halves of an indivisible whole, to be held in balance. Whoever pursues fear as a stigma and courage as an ideal will not live long. To shift responsibility and flaunt yourself as a symbol of heroism will not attract people to climb after you. The "adventure" in the travel brochure is nothing but a trick. It is to address a clien-

39

tele that wants more than they are ready for: to conquer the desire to be somebody. Real adventure means seizing opportunities, testing our strengths against the unknown, and discovering our own unique potential in the process.

A Adaptability
D Determination without conditions plus great Desire
V Vision (power of imagination) plus Values
E Experience
N Natural curiosity
T Teamwork and Trust
U Unlimited optimism
R Readiness to take Risks
E Energy, Enthusiasm, and Emotion

New Adventures

I am always trying to redirect myself. My secure existence—house, leased sports business, own Alpine school—is restricting me more and more. I do not always know how I will change myself; I only know in which direction. In doing so, I want to stay in the South Tyrol, even though I encounter more criticism and resentment here "at home." I am a South Tyrolean, even though I don't share the same standards and don't fit in. In Juval (1,000-year-old mountain ruins), I have found a place where I can spread out and unfold. I can plan, shape, and dream. My goal of having a bourgeois existence by age 40 was false. It did not correspond to my being.

Semi-Nomad

I cannot be completely myself if I cannot set out for somewhere now and then—vertically as a climber, horizontally as an ice or desert wanderer. I remain a modern semi-nomad: six months out the year at home, six months on the road. This being on the road of mine has only a few guidelines: First, I go where the others are not; second, I let myself by led by curiosity; third, I try to go to the limit; fourth, I risk coming back changed or not returning; and fifth, I follow the way of my

heart. I don't go where the media, my fans, or contract partners (publishers, sponsors) like to see me. I always go where I
could also fail. The recognition of new paths remains one of
my over-arching goals. I do not seek danger in this. It comes,
obviously, and I avoid it. It is this "going to do everything at
once," this becoming empty while walking that fulfills me.
Walking involves the whole body. And the mind. I enjoy it,
when I can walk far and long. Even afterwards, when I am
tired. I feel well, when I notice that I can walk no farther. Far
too many people do not notice where they are going.

Thinking With My Legs

The idea of exploring South Tyrol first became concrete as
a front-yard expedition. For years I have been on the trail of
our South Tyrolean self-understanding: Who are we South
Tyroleans today? What are our basic convictions? Are they
correct? As long as all people have the same opinion and think
in the same direction, it makes no difference whether we are
realists or idealists. Only in confrontations, in conflicts does
it show how far we are stuck in the rule of force. In the tiny
land of South Tyrol, where the local media can be monopo-
lized so easily, character assassination is on the agenda. In a
theoretical exchange of blows, I go as an individual, without
a lobby in the background, for a fast knockout. Only when I
think together with others and with my legs am I away from
"head people," even though they do everything together and
hide their attacks as love of the homeland, not as rising out of
the situation. I don't want to starve to death mentally in these
hoards of "Thank God" sayers and hand-shakers. All awards
and speeches of praise cannot satisfy my hunger to belong. So
I must include as many South Tyroleans as possible in
"thinking about our own land." Do we need new guiding values? Are we ready to live together peacefully? I don't want to
preach my own values. I want to tell stories and record myths
and legends—everything that comes under my feet during
my trips around the land. Deeds express more than words.

The right undertaking, animated in advance by persistence and openness, can move mountains.

Bias for Action

During our expedition to the South Wall of Lhotze in Spring 1989, I tell Hans Kammerlander about the idea of hiking around the border of South Tyrol in 40 days without rest days. He is excited and wants to come along. Even though we represent opposite political positions, I decide to do the action together in 1991. Putting an idea into action often fulfills me more than hatching the idea. Although it is difficult to set a starting day, cornerstones and the most important questions on the subject must be formulated. I make decisions according to the motto: *Better an ad hoc decision now than none at all.* Even acting chaotically is better than doing nothing in an orderly way. My attempts to delegate as many tasks as possible and to achieve results over a broad spectrum of different activities are new to me. I want stories that I have lived personally (experience). I need helpers, contributors (of information and ideas), discussion partners, and craftsmen. Testing my condition, summarizing knowledge, going on partial sections of the tour, negotiating with the media, and checking on my own promises are postponed.

For the South Tyrol hike, just as many capabilities are required as for an expedition to the Himalayas: climbing ability, endurance, persistence. In addition, there is the financing and selection of the right equipment. Also, special knowledge (about certain sections of the path and certain subjects), mountain guides, and documents must be acquired. Important and unimportant things have to be coordinated. I already have a team for this.

We want to go clockwise along the border of the South Tyrol in 40 days, without rest days. Considerations about history, politics, ecology, tourism, mountain landscapes, traffic, and future perspectives for the land are in the foreground. Day by day we gather equipment for the goal and meet with historians, priests, winegrowers, tourism strategists, natural-park experts, politicians, and local mountain guides for each section that neither Hans nor I know. I respect the independence of the these mountain guides, the individual subjects, and the people. New subjects break out spontaneously.

The regular exchange of ideas with mountain guides is important to me for two reasons: Hans and I need specialists for the most difficult sections of the path, and I want to be with and talk to as many South Tyroleans as possible. The most important thing is still that I am completely involved and committed. There is no example for either me or the others. Even a glance at recognition, which leads us all too quickly to adjusting our concepts to those of others, clouds our vision. Before I can see in a different way things that others also see, I must give up all fear of disapproval. Only in this way can I become one who truly sees.

In contrast to artists who express what they see in words, music, or pictures, I express it through my actions. Climbing is thinking with my legs. To comprehend a land and its people—and involve myself in this comprehension—is my goal. Climbing instead of talking, that is my art. It is primarily the unfalsified landscapes, no matter how useless they may seem, that permit unambiguous experiences. With my uninterrupted action, I force others to stay there and think along with me. By doing this, being unavailable to messages from the outside makes us free for messages from within.

Lust for Adventure

The reason I continue to decide for adventuring, and not for cozy evenings on a barstool, has a lot to do with quality of life. I am off again—to experience flux, change. After one adventure, I often feel a need to be inactive for a time. And from that inactivity develops a strong "lust for adventure," the desire to venture something, to expend myself to the limits of my abilities. A sense of happiness, when ideas and love of life correspond, when a mountain, a scenery begins to live.

Alive in Adventure

For some men, days on the mountains are the days when they really live. As the cobwebs in their brains get blown away, as the blood begins to course refreshingly through their veins, as all their faculties become tuned up and their whole beings become more sensitive, they detect appeals from Nature they had never heard before and see beauties that are revealed only to those who win them.

Surviving Adventure

Survival is the art of the great adventurer. He who plays the game of chance once, twice or three times and then inevitably dies is not the greatest; the border crosser who always survives is the greatest. To abort in this sense doesn't simply mean to live a few extra years. It means an increase in instincts concerning survival. It also allows freedom for other, "more reasonable" things, for new beginnings. Risk is the basic condition for an adventure, but not the goal. Without risk, adventure is inconceivable. But it does not mean dying in danger. Pulling through and surviving is the motto!

Spirit of Adventure

The person who ventures nothing gains nothing. It is unimportant whether the reason for inaction is caution or fear of failure. The panicked fear to fail slows not only the deed, but also the experience process in life, the process of becoming wise. This is why people who try and fail are dearer to me than those who hesitate, who doubt, who wait. He who is unwilling to fail makes no progress. I say with Goethe, "In the beginning was the deed."

Never Stop Exploring

The only person on whose account I could give up climbing is my mother. Previously my wife too, I admit, influenced me in critical situations, but she did not try to dissuade me from going on expeditions. And my mother, also, knows that these adventures are an expression of myself, that I have to undertake them. She is one of the very few people who really understands me. Of course she often worries, but she has sufficient confidence in me not to transmit her fears to me. Just knowing she is there, I feel stronger when I am alone, and because I know she cares, death itself does not frighten me. What I earlier felt as fear, I now perceive as love—as physical as a kind of paralysis or sigh of relief, depending on whether I am approaching a certain point of danger, or already passed it.

Excitement of Discovery

Climbing alone in unbearable conditions, I experience a strong sense of reinforced identity, as I nearly always do when I have to commit myself fully. I always feel an air of excitement when I sit beneath the summit of a mountain that I have never climbed before, and one that I am unsure whether I can climb or not. The veil of snow and the wisps of cloud blurring the summit combine to give the mountain even more of a sense of mystery. The thrill for me is not to "bag" another 8,000er, but to lift this veil.

Ambition Addiction

I have always been accused of wanting to climb without oxygen just to satisfy my ambition, but this is only partly true. I do have a fair amount of ambition, and it seems to me that I am one of the few mountaineers who stand by their ambition. In general, however, ambition leads to pretense.

"Do you still have mountaineering pipe-dreams?" In 1978, after the Nanga Parbat solo climb, I said to myself, "In the area of mountaineering, I have achieved more than I ever wanted to achieve." I had certainly dreamed of a solo ascent of an 8,000-meter mountain, and the success did my mountaineering ambition good.

"I think you are running away, or having a mid-life crisis," said a man of similar age to me in Vienna.

I responded, "If being for activity and against bureaucracy, for uncertainty and against middle-class sufficiency, for the last wild places on earth and against the exploitation of nature constitutes flight, then, gladly, I am on the run."

"And what do you do for the community?" he asked.

"Nothing," I responded. "But I love experiment and adventure. I am, therefore, a danger to this industrious, timid, and unimaginative society."

"You are passing reality by," people often say to me.

"I don't consider myself to be enlightened," I respond, "but are you sure you see reality as it actually is? I am seeking meaning, and I suppose it is immaterial what I do. The only important thing is that I remain in motion and don't become settled."

The mood of the listeners tells me that I have come up against a fundamental point there. Is it this impulse to seek, to venture the leap into the unknown, which many people perceive but so few follow? Is my generation in Europe therefore sick, because it lives in conflict, hungry for adventure but instead locked up in a little house and garden?

Strange women make me the most remarkable offers. Strange men, not likewise motivated, want me to drink a beer with them. They can all produce a reason for wanting to talk to me. I believe the main reason for it is the longing of frightened and lonely people to experience through me some fantasy in their own lives. I am confronted with loneliness and used as a substitute for what they are missing. It makes me tired and burdens me.

I cannot imagine anything more terrible than an everyday existence as it occurs in middle-class life. I know that criticism is unjust, but I am not ashamed of my refusal. The peasants in our valley have no time to think about the meaning of life. They are fully occupied doing essentials. I on the other hand am a tormented child of a generation that has to ask itself what sense there is in following an unloved profession in a world which through a materialistic mentality daily becomes more hateful. To my existence, no meaning will be given. I must find it for myself.

I have no fixed beliefs, and the passive resignation to fate of the people in my valley often drives me to despair. Only seldom can I overcome my separation from the world, can I feel myself at one with the cosmos—when I am climbing. And then only if through extreme stress, and concentration on the greatest difficulties, I reach a state in which my ego dissolves itself. To these moments, however, I am addicted.

Positive Ambition

Regretfully, ambition in central Europe is a quality with a negative connotation. But nearly everyone is ambitious. And all are allowed to be. Ambition is a part of motivation. I can only achieve optimal performance when I stand by my ambition and do what corresponds to me. And because I cannot be equally satisfied, equally well-rounded, equally happy in every phase of my life and with everything I do, it is reasonable for someone like me to change from occupation A to occupation B at this or any point in time.

In my life as an adventurer I have changed occupations at least three times: from a young, ambitious rock climber, who wanted to climb more than anything else; to a high-altitude mountain climber, who at the end had reached all 14 of the 8,000-meter peaks; then another change to an ice traveler and desert crosser. With advancing age and decreasing speed and skill, I now play mostly for perseverance, my psycho-physical strength, and for experience. I do not exclude the possibility that I will change again, when the time for such has come.

Sooner or later, almost all of my partners fell back on civil occupations; they no longer wanted to press the game between success and death. I kept playing the game for half my life, not only for practical reasons, but also because of my inclination to work with younger people. I have always connected this change with a rejuvenation. In each new playing field I addressed the young specialists and the obsessed to go one step further than was usual up to that point.

Life of Adventure

The contemplative side of climbing has become as important to me now as the necessity every so often to "push the limits." On my spring expedition in 1983, I did not just cross the boundary between China and Nepal, I transcended the boundary into a new life. The hazards encountered on a mountain, living as one with nature, had become essential to me. I was addicted to them. If I had to stay too long in Europe, I became bad-tempered. To stay alive, I needed the month-long solitude of Himalayan mountains, either alone or with a few chosen friends.

This high adventure was a half of my existence. Then, back in Europe, I was similarly happy to be among a throng of people, giving a lecture somewhere. On the one hand, I needed solitude; on the other hand, I was always glad to go back to civilization, back to "work," and to everyday stress. I am one of those people driven by ideas, who has to be active to stay physically and mentally healthy; but to generate new ideas, some pauses are necessary. I now play my life half and half—one half in the total isolation of the Himalaya, the other in the hectic rhythm of a mid-European town. I was searching for heights and depths, and needed the contrast, not just to be in mountains. The change from one extreme to another during the course of a year became so natural to me that I could go from living one day in a hotel to the next in a tent, without upset and without any sense of loss for what I had left behind.

I never experienced any contradiction in this double life, as others seem to imagine there must be. Just when I began to tire of schedules, questions, and all the bustle, I would be setting off on my travels once more. In many respects, the pace of life in Asia completely reversed the way I felt about things. My "gods" were once more the mountains, the streams, the clouds. People there regarded me with the same curiosity as I regarded them. In as much as I kept coming, it was obvious to them that I loved their land and their mountains. I adopted several of their customs: since 1981 I have worn a Xi-stone around my neck and have learned to barter with the same enthusiasm as the Khampas or Kashmiris. I am quite at home in the Himalaya. **MM**

* * *

Application and Action:

Application: Much of what people call "adventures" these days are nothing more than packaged tours. What real adventure is worth pursuing in your personal life and in your profession? How can you break out of ruts and routines and break away from your secure existence to satisfy your spirit of adventure? Might it make sense to explore, as Messner did in South Tyrol, your own front and back yard first for self-understanding? How can you cultivate a "bias for action" in yourself and team and organization? What would help you to "blow away the cobwebs in the brain?"

Action: Add a greater element of adventure to your life by putting your positive ambitions in action. Without seeking danger, decide on a certain adventure, commit to it, and do it. **AA**

Chapter 4
Happiness, Joy, and Fulfillment

What is the ultimate aim of most ventures in life? Happiness, joy, a sense of fulfillment—these are the primary drivers of our work and play, our investments of time and talent, and our faith and ambition. Messner makes the point that the happiness we desire can't be achieved in a passive mode—it is a natural byproduct of our belief in action, our persistence and performance, our experience and self-expression. We limit our enjoyment in life if we make poor use of technology and poor choices in companions and careers.

* * *

Happiness for Itself

A border-crossing, like happiness, is wanted for itself, even when it is anything but happiness. In translating my success as a mountain climber into financial success, I also succeeded in exploiting the principle of happiness. I do only what I like, even if it costs money. I use the energy feedback to prepare for new border-crossings and evaluate the old ones with an open and humble spirit. Happiness doesn't grow out of monetary savings. Happiness grows from success, from being able, from letting yourself go and reveling in your own enthusiasm. I also extract happiness from persistence in a chosen path—even obstinacy brings me joy in the progress made each day. I enjoy going high and far. I enjoy being authentic. In the border region between getting through and getting killed, everyone drops his mask very quickly. You get along only with your real face—nothing feigned. Anyone who wants to join the trip must believe in himself.

Work and Play

You are not a good-for-nothing if what you do gives you joy. Work and play are to be joined together in this life. I know that I have been privileged. Not because border crossings were lucrative, but because I can live out my "lunacies." Most people can't do that, unfortunately. How many people lose themselves in everyday things and do not do what they would like! I would be as unhappy as they, if I had to give up my form of self-expression. I feel I have not overcome being tied down and bound. I am only privileged when I do what I can do best. What we do can only be justified by our personal joy in life—never, ever in regard to material benefits. Anyone who finds his own meaning must live with the fact that the "good" and the "correct" might make him feel bad. Doubt about being alive and joy about being able to live trigger thought and action. The past and future dissolve as I act without thinking, and do what I want to do before and after.

Happiness in Achievement

Once, when arriving back at base camp, a deep feeling of happiness came over me. As a climber, I felt that I had now achieved everything—more than I ever dreamed. Now I had a story to tell. I had experienced much. To me was given the good fortune to turn my boldest dreams into reality. One man, one mountain. From now on mountains for me would be places that offer opportunities for performance. They would be natural theaters wherein I could express all my skill, my craft, and my instincts.

Enjoyment in Life

A whole new enjoyment in life opens up when we follow our dreams and climb the mountains before us. And enjoyment of life is, after all, the aim in life. We do not live simply to eat and make money. Some of us know from experience that by climbing mountains we gain some of the finest enjoyment there is in life. We like bracing ourselves against the physical difficulties the mountain presents, and feeling that we are forcing the spirit within us to prevail against the material. The challenge of altering human limitations, the delight of winning by overcoming the most extreme ordeals, the allure of having a strong relationship with nature—these motives of the Himalayan mountaineer remain the same to this day.

By our choices and use of technology, we decide ourselves in some essential—the joy, pleasure, and happiness of achieving something apparently impossible by means of our own strength and through the most extreme use of physical and psychological abilities. Today, we all live more in a world of machines and technology. On our battered planet, there is scarcely space left where we can forget our civilized society and, undisturbed, put to the test our innate powers and abilities. In us all the longing remains for primitive conditions in which we can match ourselves against nature, have the chance to have it out with her, and thereby discover ourselves. And this is the real reason that for me: There is no more fascinating challenge than this—one man and one mountain.

A Place of Fulfillment

After my solo climb of Everest, a feeling attacks me—not only a feeling of having survived or having been saved but also, little by little, I step into something that might be called a place of fulfillment, a saving haven. During the descent, I had felt infinitely melancholy—inwardly assuaged by the emotional release certainly, but at the same time depressed like the valleys under the monsoon clouds. But with each step the emotional heaviness faded little by little. With the inner easing, serenity returns, a little strength, yes even bodily well-being. By itself the fact that I can now relax is something like happiness. Like a pilgrim who has arrived at the site of the pilgrimage, I forget all the ordeals of the journey. I want to take hold of Nena and just stay there, laugh and cry, to rest myself on her and remain lying on the glacier. Immobile, without a word I stand there, as fragile as a light bulb. A single word would suffice to destroy this glassy delicacy, this strange envelope, which is all that is left of me. I can see through all my layers and know that I am also transparent for Nena. Leaning on the ski sticks, I stare at her a while. Then I break down. All my reserve is gone. I weep. It is as if all horizons, all boundaries are broken. Everything is revealed; all emotions are released.

Climbing for Pleasure

Climbing mountains must provide pleasure—how often have I heard that notion, ever since I was a schoolboy. But the fact that our climbing trips on Sundays were more strenuous and tiring than the entire work week did not affect me. Also, I received nothing for climbing a mountain. But tiredness is not the critical thing, nor is the compensation. It is the enthusiasm, the joy in the thing. As a border-crosser, I live *for* my undertakings, and not *from* them, even though my border crossings feed me indirectly as I can live from the "byproducts." Nevertheless, I am anything but an idealist. I am a realist who knows real joy.

Happiness in Doing

And what is absolute enthusiasm, pure pleasure, and enduring joy other than being possessed with the desire of your heart! I demand much more of myself in my voluntary pursuit of climbing. Anyone who is not possessed by the thing he is doing, will find less happiness in it—and likewise less success. Enthusiasm and success go hand in hand: in sports, in science, in art. The same applies to work, to the extent that it is described as such when we build it into this principle of happiness. Happiness does not grow by saving it but by sharing it.

Joy in Your Own Way

I feel it is less important to learn how to do a job by the prescribed method than to find your own way. Your path does not appear on your birth certificate. You cannot learn it in school. Your parents cannot bring it out of you. You must seek this path for yourself. In making your own path and finding success, you experience not only the joy of being able to get through, but also the spiritual high from your innovations and creations.

Breath of Happiness

Standing now in diffused light, with the wind at my back, I experience suddenly a feeling of completeness—not a feeling of having achieved something or of being stronger than everyone who was ever here before, not a feeling of having arrived at the ultimate point, not a feeling of supremacy. Just a breath of happiness deep inside my mind and my soul. MM

❋   ❋   ❋

Application and Action:

Application: The essence of Messner's life and message is his insistence on authentic self-expression, the "signature" approach to life, that makes of people not cogs in a big machine but personalities with unique perspectives—individuals with character and competence who sign their names to their work and thereby reap an extra measure of joy, meaning, and fulfillment from their work and play. In your application of Messner's principle of happiness, look for opportunities to express your ideas and talents in an authentic manner.

Action: Create your own plan of happiness and consider how you might expend your personal plan to have a positive impact on the people you live and work with. **AA**

Summit Climb in a Snowstorm
by Oswald Oelz, climber of two 8,000ers

The monsoon storm tears at my little tent, pitched on a flat bit of ice at 7,000 meters and anchored with ice screws and my climbing axe. Every time a huge gust of wind catches it, I expect to be blown away. I think about Reinhold and Friedl, who must also be sitting out the storm in their tent, 100 meters above me. And I'm thinking, "We are going to have to give up and go home, leaving Shisha Pangma as unfinished business."

But about 5 o'clock in the evening, half-asleep, I hear my name being called above the howl of the wind. Two ice-encrusted figures arrive in front of my tent: Reinhold and Friedl, leaning on their ski sticks. Reinhold gasps, "We've been to the top—in this! We left early this morning. Friedl was dead set on giving it a try. This was a big day for him. He broke trail most of the way—it was murder."

It must have been. Their haggard faces appeared almost green above their icy beards. In this incredible storm, they had to climb over 1,000 vertical meters to reach the summit. And they lived to tell the tale! Anyone else would be sitting in the snow somewhere by now, sleeping—perhaps forever.

From somewhere Reinhold is able to summon up sufficient energy to press on. He wants us down in Advanced Base Camp tonight. Without skis, he keeps sliding, then sitting in the snow, unable to stay on his feet. But he always gets up and goes on. About 1 o'clock in the morning, we stagger into camp.

An overwhelming urge to break taboos and climb in that border region between life and death has already led Reinhold into other critical situations, on Nanga Parbat and Manaslu, as well as on his two solo ascents of Nanga Parbat and Everest. It has made him into one of the few survivors of high-altitude mountaineering.

When he started this game in 1970, Reinhold brought to it all the right physical prerequisites: he had grown up in the mountains, his body and mind had been toughened on many of the hardest tours in the Alps; he was the leading Alpinist of the late sixties.

Scientists and others have shown great interest in his psychological characteristics. Before his historic climb of Everest without oxygen, various professors and pundits, believing they knew more about it than Reinhold did, declared that the attempt would fail, or at the very least would lead to severe brain damage. When no intellectual impairment could be discerned in either Messner or Habeler after their Everest adventure, the line was then taken that they must both be unusually able to take up oxygen and make economic use of it. However, in all aspects of oxygen uptake and use, Reinhold falls within the normal physiological limits of any athletes who engage in sports that require staying power and good training.

The secret of Reinhold's mountaineering success does not lie in any exceptional physical capabilities, apart from his ability to assess a situation shrewdly. Rather it lies in his motivation and in his capacity to endure hardship and pain, allowing him to overcome barriers that are rather more psychological than physiological. Messner has exploded other myths, as he did the one that man could not live above 8,500 meters without an oxygen mask. The impetus that drives him is an alert spirit, open to fantasies and readily ignited by taboos and barriers. The same aggressiveness and relentlessness that Reinhold displays when attacking real and imagined opponents or problems, he can also turn upon himself, whenever success or survival demand it.

Thus, he has become the principal player in the "Sufferings Game," having pushed his body and mind to the uttermost limits of endurance. This is something Nena saw on his return from his solo ascent of Everest; he was totally played out, drained to his very soul. And I, too, observed it when he and Friedl came down off Shisha Pangma. But exhausted as he was, Reinhold was still capable of drawing new strength from somewhere.

Section II

* * *

Goals and Success

Many inactive and passive people rely on extrinsic motivation—forces outside themselves —to act upon them before they start in motion. They are living proof of the physics law of motion: A body at rest tends to remain at rest—unless acted upon by some outside force. Messner has been a dynamic body in motion, and hence he has remained in motion, and motivated largely by forces from within. In this section, he relates how goals—dreams with deadlines—directly and indirectly, stimulate the activities of getting started, making progress, gaining experience, and reaching the summit: the path to real success.

Chapter 5

Motivation and Goals

The difference between Messner's method for setting and meeting goals and the way we might approach a New Year's resolution is day and night. First, we note the depth of his resolution, determination, and commitment. His motivation comes not from the outside but comes as "momentum from the inside." He makes the greatest demands on himself. He sets goals to bring out the best in himself, step by step. When motivating others, he is careful not to manipulate them unnecessarily. In seeking his goals of going as high and as far as possible, he finds ethical ways to enlist the energy of others in cooperative, win-win ventures.

* * *

The Power of Goals

When I set a goal to climb Everest without an oxygen mask, Alpine style, I was determined to climb until I either reach the top of the mountain, or I can go no further. I feel so passionately about this that I am prepared to endure just about anything, to risk much. I am willing to go further than ever I have before. I am resolved, for this idea, to stake everything I have. I have made up my mind to climb Everest, in much the same way as someone might decide to write a book or stitch a garment. And I am prepared for anything I might have to face on my way to the summit. During the walk in to Base Camp, I frequently asked myself why I should want to climb Everest without oxygen. The reason does not lie in a pure mountaineering or sporting purpose. To explain this I have to turn back to history and say that in the first 200 years of alpine climbing, the mountain was the important thing. During this time it was the summit that was conquered and explored— that was the unknown that man attempted to reach by any means, employing any techniques. But for some years now and particularly on my own tours, it is no longer the mountain that is important, but the man—the man with the critical situations met on high mountains, with solitude, with altitude.

Primary and Secondary Goals

Having climbed all 14 of the 8,000-meter peaks in the world—and having stood atop an 8,000-meter mountain 18 times—I don't feel especially heroic, not even exceptional as a climber. I have merely seen a task through to completion— a goal I had set for myself years before. I am pleased to be done with it. If it means I "won the race," then I am pleased to be done with that, too—and all the people who make such capital out of it. It is all behind me at last. I can now start living the rest of my life. I feel light and free. The whole world lay before me. It had taken me 16 years to climb all 14 mountains. But that hadn't been the object in the beginning, and even if it later became a goal, it was only a secondary one.

I did not "collect" 8,000ers, as my critics have suggested. Not even in 1982, when I succeeded in climbing three 8,000-meter mountains in one season. But it was after this first 8,000-meter "hat trick" that I decided to climb all 14 of them. It was not simply to bring the list to an end. The purpose of all my 8,000-meter climbs has been to work through an idea. Of far greater importance to me was climbing increasingly harder routes, setting new targets for myself, looking for new ways to tackle problems, and pushing the limits of my climbing, and myself, ever further.

MOTIVATION AND GOALS

Self-Motivation

The difference between sportsmen and border-crossers is the difference between science and adventure. A border-crosser goes because it is dangerous. A scientist who travels in the Antarctic, even though it is dangerous, will do everything to avoid potential dangers. The border-crosser will exploit them. I have adopted the motto, *"Vinciturus vincero,"* a Latin proverb painted over the main door of the great hall in my city of Juval in South Tyrol. This was one of my motives for acquiring this desolate property in 1983. *"Victurus vicero"* (Classical Latin) can be translated in various ways: "Whoever decides on victory will be victorious." But also: "Who sees himself as a conqueror, will conquer." Or: "The one who is determined to win, will win." In all these translations, and probably also in the original meaning, this Latin proverb makes the clear statement that *motivation is momentum from the inside.* There is no greater stimulation for one's own enthusiasm than self-determination. This critical dimension of self-motivation includes mind, spirit, and body. It controls the will, stokes an "inner fire," and lets us go do things completely. The thing called "flow" in the "zone" can arise only in this way: You are fully concentrating on your task, comfortably relaxed, full of energy, and no longer thinking about anything else. The dimension of time is completely suspended. This self-motivation has nothing to do with either egotism or idealism—it stands outside both of them.

Making Demands on Ourselves

I am not an idealist. I try to be a realist. Beyond that, I am an egotist. I have made myself known for my egotism. And everyone who does not do what he does—as a pedestrian, seller, head of state, or TV moderator—with enthusiasm, should not reproach me. He should change his life. We are all entitled to our egotism, if we make demands on ourselves and not on others. It is neither more nor less virtuous to live one's life rather than depend on some kind of ideal. Motivation does not fall from heaven. It is hidden in all of us. It only has to be awakened. Each motivation is tailored to the individual. So if we want to infect or motivate another person with our enthusiasm, we must get into him. We must first know this other person.

Goals Bring Out the Best in Us

In setting goals, I am not just organizing my life—I am, once and for all, seeking success. Greater respect for a goal brings out the best in me. After my solo hike of Mount Everest from the north (August 1980) and a Shish-Pangma expedition (May 1981), my ambition to climb high mountains was satisfied for a season.

Three in One

Once I had climbed three 8,000-meter peaks, the possibility of achieving all 14 peaks more than 8,000-meters above sea level became conceivable. A completely new cost-benefit analysis was available: training, acclimatization, and financing. There were multiple possibilities to be evaluated. The idea of climbing three 8,000-meter (26,247-foot) mountains on a single trip comes from a young mountain-climber: Friedl Mutschlechner. "Overcoming the useless," as the Frenchman Lionel Terray called extreme mountain climbing, suddenly makes sense. To climb three 8,000-meter peaks in a row, means not only a series of efforts, but also multiplied success.

Motivation or Manipulation?

Motivation can also be manipulation. The question arises: "To what extent we should influence others for the sake of reaching our goals?" I have often been able to push my partners toward my goals with tricks, with good persuasion, as if those goals were their own. Faking false facts is lying. But it is part of a survival strategy. It helps in manipulating the motivation of others in such a way that their behavior changes to their own advantage. All leaders do this to some degree. They subject people to pressure to succeed. This is characteristic of leaders of our time, for whom only the result of our efforts counts—not the learning process. If I apply civil standards to this "manipulative" behavior, I may be breaking the limits of what is permitted by law. And the people I lead may think of me as a military policeman because I do not care about conventions, only about "success." And so my style may not fit well into the world view. But I respect limits and the other person, even when I manipulate him; again, I honor the laws of nature.

Moreover, I have never met a "genuine person, helpful and good." The moral systems in a world of egotists are more or less successful attempts to hide one's own egotism at the expense of others. Even though it is always more advantageous to present yourself as more truthful, helpful, and better than you really are, I still attempt to present my experiences and myself unembellished.

The solution to this leadership dilemma of motivation vs. manipulation is to be found in two opposite directions: in refusing and in creating. Two people who are opposed to each other influence or restrain themselves. So many of my expeditions would have failed if I had not used rhetorical tricks. In the Antarctic or Greenland, no one can be left behind. If one person gives up, all must give up. If one person has no more desire, it costs all the others their success. In a small team, everything depends on each individual. Consideration of all the many incalculable risks that are involved in the adventure is less important than the motivation (and manipulation) of the partners. Not everyone can be influenced through reason. But on the subconscious levels, which we can influence for a short time, there is a memory for success. For example, when I started up on my solo trip on Mount Everest, although I had intended to climb down after falling into a crevasse, the motivation was stronger than the short-term decision to give up. A counter-example: When I tried in 1973 to climb Nanga Parbat alone, I was as well prepared as possible. I therefore wanted to go forward when the first crisis occurred on the wall. There was no rational reason to turn back. Although I wanted to climb upwards, I climbed downward. I let it happen. For I am not stubborn enough to place my reasoning over my subconscious decisions.

Motivation is like bottled, concentrated energy. It is stored for a long time as expectation, hope, and dedication. Only when a goal is filled with passion does it become independent. Our motivation then seeks an outlet, no matter what the price. Often motivation plays itself out more through feelings than through reason. The half of the brain that I must address for motivation is not the same as the one that works out planning and logistics.

In larger expeditions in the Himalayas, I can find the motivated partners for an 8,000-meter peak before the climb. Less-motivated people can climb with us for a way or wait in the base camp. Anyone who doesn't want to stay at all, goes. I have never forced anyone on a Himalaya expedition to stay on to the end. Often, one or another has gone home earlier or stayed in the base camp without being interested in the summit.

The Goal of Going as Far as Possible

In the autumn of 1980—after achieving the high point of my life as a mountain climber—to climb "as high as possible" (Mount Everest solo trip without outside help and oxygen masks)—a vague goal surfaced to go "as far as possible" — a crossing of Antarctica. But this goal was postponed indefinitely in 1982, after I decided to climb all 14 of the 8,000-meter peaks.

In December 1986, a few moths after the Lhotse ascent (my last 8,000-meter climb), I traveled with two friends to Antarctica to climb Mount Vinson (the highest mountain in Antarctica, one of the seven summits). The idea of an Antarctic crossing becomes a real utopia.

At the site, I test ability to go on skis with fur coats and to pull various heavy sleds. In one hour I go 4 kilometers (2.5 miles) with a 100-kilo (220-pound) sled. In eight hours of pure hiking per day, I can therefore make 30 kilometers (18.6

miles) a day. In 100 days—this is how long the Antarctic summer lasts—3,000 kilometers (1,860 miles). The route by which Sir Ernest Shackleton planned his 1914 crossing of Antarctica (failed, because his ship "Endurance" was crushed between ice flows during the approach) could be achieved in about three months.

After Adventure Network had promised logistic support (approach, flying in two depots), I establish the cornerstones of my strategy: two or three men, sleds weighing 100 kilos, hike without dogs or pulling machines, from the Ronne shelf ice, across the South Pole, to McMurdo. A strong momentum for the crossing of Antarctica arises.

Meeting the Goal Together

In the Antarctic, I could have continued the expedition alone, but I wanted to have my partner (Arved Fuchs) with me to the end for two reasons: for safety reasons and because we had started out as a pair. I did not want to appear before our public as one who "goes over a dead body." We got along for 92 days without a serious dispute, even though each of us was capable of absorbing the weak motivation or motivating power of the other.

Arved Fuchs and I finally had success in the Antarctic, although as two very different characters who did not fit well together. We had success because we always understood how to add to each other's abilities. Whether it was motivation or manipulation, we did not give up on supporting each other, bringing each other together. It is true that there was unrest between us, but without disputation. This finally led to success, in which braking and lubricating roles were equally important. As individuals, we would both have failed in the Antarctic. But as a team, we went farther on foot than all others before us. We met our goal of going as far as possible.

Cooperation

Fellow travelers are like dinner companions. They understand the art of attracting the most attention possible with the least effort possible. The larger the group, the more difficult cooperation becomes. Much sensitivity is needed to motivate different characters. With us border-crossers, self-motivation and the ability to bring a partner out of lethargy, fatigue, and hopelessness are what count primarily.

To what extent our self-motivation comes from inside as enthusiasm for a goal or from outside as pressure to perform is difficult to distinguish. And it cannot be measured. I know that all of us seek and need the recognition of others. We are thus heteronomous—interdependent up to a certain point. Seen in this way, we are always under pressure to perform, to the extent that we respect others, outsiders, in any way.

I know that *the strongest motivations come from the inner depths of the soul*. The hope of fame and money are not sufficient to support a person up to his personal performance limit. I can explain my successes not only in terms of my will to perform but also in terms of simply giving in to my enthusiasm and sometimes also to the expectations of others. No matter how much I try not to get caught up in pressure to perform, I have never succeeded completely and permanently in shaking off all heteronomy. With a surface motivation, however, I achieve only a low momentum; with too little energy at the end, perhaps, to accomplish a major goal.

Sometimes there is an over-motivation in my action, perhaps because of pressure to perform or because of time becoming shorter with increasing age. Motivation is associated with the ability to inspire enthusiasm and give meaning and with visions. But over-motivation leads to paralysis and cramping, sometimes to catastrophe. Wanda Rutkiewicz, for example, the most successful female mountain-climber of the last two decades—she has climbed eight of the 14 8,000-meter peaks—wanted to climb the rest of the 8,000-meter peaks she had not reached in a series. With great attention to publicity, she started out. In this, she no longer had the speed and endurance of a 30-year old. She was surely experienced and motivated. But she was under time pressure. And perhaps because of this pressure placed on her, she became paralyzed—she was killed in the spring of 1992 on the north side of Kangchendzönga, the third-highest mountain in the world. This tragedy is lunacy: her willpower and experience were enough to allow her to get so high that no one could then bring her back down alive.

When the game becomes to go as far as possible, to climb as high as possible, to a forced "must," it is a doubly dangerous game. "As far as possible" is also dangerous in business, sports, and politics. Every time it is taken seriously. There are limits that we have to respect. Anyone who wants to jump over these limits is gambling—like an industrialist with distorting the environment, like a sportsman with drugs sometimes, like a border-crosser with death.

Motivation to Reach Goals

To what extent my goals were influenced from the outside can be seen in my ability to make judgments. Not only the experience of performance, but also the pressure to perform—from outside and inside—to which all of us are subject, forces us, others and ourselves, to demonstrate something over and over again: how courageous, how enduring, how "good" we are. It remains difficult for each individual to separate the pressure to perform from the will to perform. Again, whoever decides to win, will win. Once I set a goal for myself, a creative impatience arises. Motivation cannot be driven, whipped, or injected. I need only weigh the apparently impossible to mobilize forces that I had not imagined. **MM**

*   *   *

Application and Action:

Application: How can you tap into the power of internal motivation to meet your goals? In this chapter, Messner gives us many ideas that have broad application to personal and professional challenges. For example, in setting his goal to climb Everest without oxygen, he pledges to prepare and endure and risk all, short of sacrificing his life, to reach the summit. His goal to climb all 14 of the 8,000-meter peaks is made with the motive to push the limits of his climbing and himself. "The one who is determined to win, will win," he reminds us. He set a goal to climb three peaks in one expedition to gain leverage and economies of motion and scale.

Action: In setting goals that are meaningful to you, especially ones that may appear to some people to be "impossible" or "useless," explore the inner depths of your soul to discover the strongest motivations, the noblest motives, and the fairest means for reaching the summit, either alone or in the company of others who share the dream.   **AA**

Chapter 6

Getting Started and Acclimated

The old cliche, "The journey of 1,000 miles starts with the first step," certainly applies to climbing 8,000-meter mountains. Messner makes a powerful point of taking that first step, of getting started and acclimated, even when you don't have all the answers. Any great mountain is like a giant jigsaw puzzle with many unknowns. Apprehension makes starting the climb harder. But Messner gladly accepts the responsibility to first get himself started. He enters the thin air of high altitude with a positive attitude, trusting in his body's ability to acclimatize and cope with the stresses. He believes that the body even has a memory for high altitude. Still, in extreme conditions, he must exercise the power of positive self-talk, faith, and belief to overcome the debilitating forces of fear and inertia.

❋   ❋   ❋

Getting Started

At age 20 or 25, everyone starts on an adventure that is over his head. Who has not, at least once in life, assumed the most extreme risk? But growing older means, among other things, becoming weaker and more cautious. Still, embarking on a great feat means placing all experience in the balance. Primarily experience, instincts, and knowledge have the desire to be confirmed.

Approaching a Big Mountain

Like a jigsaw puzzle, Mount Everest comes together. The

mountain builds itself up from its walls, glaciers, and ridges. In a moment its contours are as familiar to me as if I had always lived here. Ghost-like, as in a dream, I experience the visible reality. The mountain seems to grow as I gaze toward it. Ever more mightily it towers up before me; far above the summit appears dark. I cannot see the glaciers at its foot for they are hidden behind the hills.

Shivers go through my body, although I do not find the mountain terrifying. I stand before one of my former loves, whose power of attraction is still a puzzle to me. My senses are over-strung, worn down by the strain of the long approach journey and no longer capable of processing quickly enough the impressions that assail me.

The first real approach to a big mountain is always exciting. There are so many unknowns: the weather, the possible course of the route—the way I will react in the face of this self-imposed task. Every time Mount Everest becomes visible, I am seized by a feeling of hopelessness, a whole new experience of weakness bordering on impotence.

Getting Myself Started

When I am free for a new project, I begin anew the familiar cycle of getting started. Even though more than half of my life is over, I still make demands on myself. But I no longer ask myself why. Only when I am possessed by an idea do I start out. Then I am not interested in either profit or loss; curiosity is still my primary driving force. I do not place myself in the coffin of remembering the past; I know how to get myself started, even in the middle of Europe. I know much less than I guess. I put guesses to the hardest test. Anyone who wants to go high or go far, wants to do it on his own two feet. No "rope trail" leads to the highest peaks. How often have I thought ahead to a border-crossing without being forced to do so. I have read the reports, diaries, and accounts of my predecessors—not like novels, but as technical literature. I have mixed these materials with own experiences and internalized them. This is not genius. It is simply anticipation and preparation for what lies ahead.

Thin Air

At great heights, climbers frequently notice a lack of clarity of thought. Of course it is hard for a dulled brain to recognize stupidity, but still I hold it not impossible that Everest climbers try to drink their food, go backwards, or do other comic things. In thin air, it is not only hard to think clearly, it is also extremely difficult to suppress the desire to do nothing. If something were able to rob us of success, then in first place I would put the lack of will-power caused by oxygen starvation.

Extreme Altitudes

At extreme altitudes, after climbing 30 or 40 meters, I have to rest. I am still not sufficiently acclimatized and cannot yet rightly see how I am to cope with the stresses higher up. The air is thin. I keep trying to breathe deeply. When I am well acclimatized, I no longer have the feeling of being short of breath when I exert myself. After seven weeks at an altitude of more than 5,000 meters, I run around in base camp as if I were at home. You accustom swiftly to the rarefied air if you have already been at great heights. For newcomers, it is harder. During my later expeditions, I had less trouble than on my first. On my earlier expeditions, I sometimes experienced a feeling of paralysis, of insecurity; those deep moments of despair when suddenly you have no more strength. The body seems to become inured not only through frequent repetitions—it also develops a sort of memory for it, adapting itself more easily. But even that takes three or four weeks and is progressive. Without first making these adjustments, reaching the summit of Everest would be unthinkable, even if you previously climbed all the 8,000-meter mountains. This adjustment to altitude is fundamental to the ascent. But I don't see it as a preparation. Just as I must wait for better weather, so I wait for the best bodily state.

Self-talk to Reach a Goal

I lack nothing, the forthcoming climbing problems are well within my capabilities, and yet I must force myself to believe in success. I know that I can do it. Nevertheless I need to talk myself into not giving up. I need so much energy just to fight against fear and inertia. In this I pursue a goal which only climbers can understand. When shall I finally be able to live without a goal? Why do I myself stand in the way with my ambition and fanaticism? From the back of my mind springs one fragment of thought after another, to and fro, like points of condensed energy, finding no way out, with a life of their own, as if there were an energy in my field of force which is independent of me. Indeed it belongs to me, but exists without my so much as lifting a finger, without impulse. Even in sleep, it comes and goes against my will. So it is also with this almost tangible power around me. A spirit breathes regularly in and out, which originates from nothingness and which condenses to nothingness. Only somewhere between these extreme forms do I perceive it, even with my senses.

Prepare to Start

I am not one of the wonder-men who, like yogis in the Himalayas, can lower their heart rate or their body temperature at will. I have also not trained my muscles to use a minimum amount of oxygen. I had already climbed two 8,000-meter peaks before—both without oxygen equipment—and accumulated my experiences in that process. That was all. It is certain that the vegetative nervous system can be influenced by training, self-control, and thinking ahead. All this, however, I did unconsciously. Perhaps I suspected that thoughts strengthened by feelings have more energy. I knew that I must not become ill, and trust in my companions. In every respect, I have only become ill once on a large trip, as if the strengthening of my immune system were an accompanying step to the high mood when starting out. Being underway in the border region has always made me healthier than I was at home. **MM**

* * *

Application and Action:

Application: Sometimes the hardest part is just getting started, taking the first few steps of faith into unknown or foreboding territory. In these few entries, Messner bids us to take those steps with him, to experience for ourselves the unique sensation of beginning with the end in mind but not knowing how the venture will turn out. Read extensively between the few lines he gives about the need for acclimation and find applications as you ascend to new heights. Observe his word of caution: "Without first making these adjustments, reaching the summit would be unthinkable." Again, Messner operates in harmony with natural law: the law of progression, the law of learning and adapting along the way.

Action: Take the first bold step toward a summit you have imagined for yourself. Spend some time getting acclimated to the altitude, to the "rarefied air" of the unknown territory. Learn the ropes. But above all, be underway. **AA**

Chapter 7

Making Progress and Gaining Experience

Along the way, once underway, making progress and gaining personal knowledge and experience are all important. You have to care less about image and more about imagination and innovation and initiative—and the humility to begin at the beginning and build from there. Once on the face, you calm down, doubts fade, resolve builds, and the "impossible" become doable. You begin to see even repeated "failures" and the need to occasionally back down or wait out a storm as mere delays or obstacles to inevitable success. The ultimate "trick," notes Messner, is simply this: to fail, learn, and start over; to fall, reflect, and rise again— to keep moving, to keep going on—drawing on experience, hope, confidence, curiosity, and cosmic energy to endure to the end.

* * *

Personal Experience

Personal experience is the most important thing along the way. It is always individual. There are many ways to personal experience, but fundamentally only two directions: the physical and the psychical. Both ways are correct, both are important. You cannot teach a person to be at peace. You cannot buy joy in life, even though it is offered everywhere. Even existence experience is not given to us. You must experience all of this yourself. I can do it best in the wilderness. I am composed of many wonderful memories because of my many wonderful experiences.

Gaining Experience

In Greenland, when I was stuck at the beginning of the winter crossing in new-fallen snow, this belief that I "didn't make it" equaled a loss of image. But it did not encumber me. The loss of image means less to me than does gaining experience. And experience comes with failure. It is important to repeatedly realize that we are limited, especially in relation to the forces of nature. Experiences with the expeditions would not be possible, if I were not limited—limited in my energy, limited in my strength, limited in my courage, and limited in my experience. In the conflict with a wild natural world, experiences are only possible because I am limited. Therefore, I never have problems choosing failure and continued life.

The realization that I should advance only "to this point and no further"comes spontaneously, often in fractions of a second. And I yield to it. During our first attempt to climb the southeast wall of the Cho Oyo in the Himalayas during winter, I looked briefly at my partner, Hans Kammerlander. We were nearly to the peak and had just plodded onto an avalanche-ready snow slope. We did not speak a word. But I knew that he too believed it best to turn back. The dangers were excessive: the slope could have given and dragged us with it at even the smallest vibration. We would rather descend, rather lose face, than possibly meet death.

On the Face

Once on the face, climbing, I calm down. If I make progress, however slow, if I see I am rising to meet the difficulties, then the doubts fade away—they have no place any more. Only sometimes, when I have to wait about, and in the tent, do they come back. The knowledge that I can endure cold, and thrive on climbing into the wind doesn't help at all. But once I am out of my sleeping bag in the morning, all these worries and doubts disappear. They hardly ever make an appearance when I am actually climbing, even when things are not going well and there is no knowing how they will end—even when the climb seems to uphold the law that risks increase in proportion with height.

Making Progress

I will have to begin from the beginning if I want to go on from here. I have to learn it all again. In any different field, I have to master what has already been done to take a step forward, in the same way as everyone who has gone before me. My life takes a new direction. So long as I am criticized by older and younger climbers, I am reassured. I know I am on the right path and making progress.

Fail and Start Over

The idea of "all 14 of the 8,000-meter peaks" motivated me as a high-mountain climber. Not until 1986, after repeated failures, was I able to succeed in this. To fail and start over and over again for 16 long years—this was a key to this success. I experimented for a long time with styles, financing, and partners in order to find my most promising working method. In the end, I mixed styles and combined various tactics. A successful border-crossing is rare—and useless—like gold.

Fall and Rise Again

At times along the way, I am so tired and so relieved when I finally decide to stop. The awareness that no further effort is required for the day works wonders to restore hope and strength. Was it not myself, but a power from without which drove me on? I feel it to be so. My will returns to normal, and I begin to think clearly again. I can perceive again, not merely see. After falling or resting, I am able to rise again.

A Driving Unrest at Everest

I feel a driving unrest in my innermost being. It is not fear that suddenly seizes me like a big all-embracing hand. It is all the experiences of my mountaineering life that spread out in me and press for activity. The exertion of 30 years of climbing—the avalanches I have survived and the states of exhaustion I have experienced—have condensed over the decades to a feeling of deep helplessness. Nonetheless, I must go on! Time won is never saved. I know what can happen to me during the next few days as I approach a summit. I know how great the grind will become just below the summit. This knowledge is only endurable in physical activity.

I Must Go On

I must go on, and yet each small chore is an effort. Up here life is brutally racked between exhaustion and will-power; self-conquest becomes a compulsion. Why don't I go down? There is no occasion to continue. But I cannot simply give up without reason. I wanted to make the climb. I still want to. What drives me on to the summit of Everest? Is it curiosity (where is Mallory?), the game (man versus Mount Everest), ambition (I want to be the first)? No, all these superficial incentives vanished at some point. Whatever it is that drives me is planted much deeper than I or the magnifying glass of the psychologists can detect. Day by day, hour by hour, minute by minute, step by step I force myself to do something against which my body rebels. At the same time this condition is only bearable in activity. Only a bad omen or the slightest illness would be a strong excuse for me to descend.

Cosmic Energy

The weather is fine. Tomorrow I shall be on the summit! The moment I crawl out of the tent, my confidence is back once more—as if I am breathing cosmic energy. Or is it only the summit with which I identify? The air above me seems to be thin, of that soft blue that looks transparent. The mountains below me I see only as wavy surfaces, a relief in black and white. Take down the tent, fold it up! I command myself. But now these impulses no longer come from the mind; they come from the gut. Each drawing of breath fills my lungs with air, fills my being with self-realization. There can be no doubt.

Now or Never

I am not at this moment under threat. It is all so peaceful here around me. I am not in any hurry. I cannot go any faster. I submit to this realization as to a law of nature. I think only of going on. As if retreat, failure, had never crossed my mind. But what if the mist becomes thicker? Ought I to wait a bit? No, that is senseless. In any case I am already very late. I must get outside. At this height there is no recovering. By tomorrow I could be so weak that there would not be enough left for a summit bid. It's now or never. I must either go up or go down. There is no other choice. Nevertheless, the voices in the air are there again. I don't ask myself where they come from. I accept them as real. In spite of the enormous strain which each step upwards requires, I am still convinced that I shall get to the top, which I experience now in a sort of anticipation, like a deliverance.

An Inspiring Hope

The knowledge of being half-way there in itself soothes me, gives me strength, drives me on. Often I am near the end of my tether. After a dozen paces everything in me screams to stop, sit, breathe. But after a short rest I can go on. Worrying about the weather costs me additional energy. And the ever-recurring question of the descent. But simultaneously in the thickening mist I experience an inspiring hope, something like curiosity outside of time and space—not the demoralizing despair which a visible and unendingly distant summit triggers.

It Must Be!

It is now all about the struggle against my own limitations. This becomes obvious with each step; with each breath it resolves itself. The decision to climb up or down no longer bothers me. It is the irregular rhythm, the weakness in the knees. I go on like a robot. Against all bodily remonstrances, I force myself upwards. It must be! I don't think much. I merely converse with myself to cheer myself up. My only adversary is the slope; time no longer exists. I consist of tiredness and exertion.

I Keep Moving

I guess myself to be near the top, but the knife edge goes on forever. During the next three hours I am aware of myself no more. I am one with space and time. Nevertheless, I keep moving. Every time the blue sky shows through the thick clouds, I believe I see the summit; I believe I am there. But still there are snow and stones above me. The few rocks which rise out of the snow are greeny-grey, shot through here and there with brighter streaks. Ghostlike they stir in the wispy clouds. For a long time I traverse upwards, keeping to the right. A steep rock barrier bars the way to the ridge. Only if I can pass the wall to the right shall I get any higher.

Where Is the Summit?

Arriving on the crest of the Northeast Ridge, I sense the cornices. I stand still. Then I lie down on the snow. Now I am there. The ridge is flat. Where is the summit? Groaning I stand up again, stamp the snow down. With ice axe, arms and upper body burrowing in the snow, I creep on, keeping to the right. Ever upwards.

When I rest I feel utterly lifeless except that my throat burns when I draw breath. Suddenly it becomes brighter. I turn round and can see down into the valley, right to the bottom where the glacier flows. Breathtaking! Automatically I take a few photographs. Then everything is all grey again. Completely windless.

I Can Scarcely Go On

Once more I must pull myself together. I can scarcely go on. No despair, no happiness, no anxiety. I have not lost the mastery of my feelings; there are actually no more feelings. I consist only of will. After each few meters, this too fizzles out in an unending tiredness. Then I think nothing, feel nothing. I let myself fall, just lie there. For an indefinite time I remain completely irresolute. Then I make a few steps again.

At most it can only be another 10 meters up to the top! To the left below me project enormous cornices. For a few moments I spy through a hole in the clouds the North Peak far below me. Then the sky opens out above me too. Oncoming shreds of cloud float past nearby in the light wind. I see the grey of the clouds, the black of the sky, and the shining white of the snow surface as one. They belong together like the stripes of a flag. I must be there.   **MM**

*   *   *

Application and Action:

Application: In this chapter, Messner places high value on gaining experience and making progress, albeit slow and painful at times. He recognizes that falls and failures may spell the end of the day or even signal the end of an expedition, but if you can survive you can use that raw experience to excel on a subsequent attempt. As you near the summit, expect fierce restraining forces and opposition. Indeed, the final few steps up—and even the descent back down—may require you to expend the last ounce of strength and will and resource available to you.

Action: In your quest for the summit, document what you are learning to make the experience more worthwhile to you and to those who may follow you. Document the personal cost of your progress and accomplishment.   **AA**

Chapter 8
Reaching the Summit

When at last we reach the summit after much struggle and sacrifice, how sweet are the emotions. A flood of feeling may fill our souls. We hear music, a symphony, although we may well be in a state of physical exhaustion and spiritual abstraction. We may also feel a wave of happiness or relief wash over us, even though we still sense tension—teetering between earth and sky, ascent and descent. Messner even wonders if he has, in some way, become the summit. He makes a strong argument, since the greatest victory is victory over self.

✳   ✳   ✳

Nothing But Sky

Above me, nothing but sky. I sense it, although in the mist I see as little of it as the world beneath me. In the mist, in the driving of the clouds, I cannot see at first whether I am really standing on the highest point. It seems almost as if the mountain continues on up to the right. But perhaps that only seems so, perhaps I deceive myself. No sign of my predecessors. It is odd that I cannot see the Chinese aluminum survey tripod that has stood on the summit of Everest since 1975. Suddenly I am standing in front of it. I take hold of it, grasp it like a friend. It is as if I embrace my opposing force, something that absolves and electrifies at the same time. At this moment I breathe deeply. This tripod, which rises now scarcely knee-high out of the snow, triggers off no sort of euphoria in me. It is just there.

85

Summit Feelings

When you reach a summit—when there's no more up—
you stand up there, wanting nothing more than to be safely
back down on flat ground, where it's warm; back down where
it is possible to rest; down where your friends are waiting. In
this almost airless void, no one lasts long. It is not just that
there is insufficient oxygen; there is also too little human
warmth, too little sense, too little love. I very quickly become
worn down up there, unlike anything at lower levels.

I spend only a few minutes on high summits because I
know that the sort of luck I seek there, on the summit—good
weather, little wind, strength, safety, and sanity—only exists
at lower altitudes.

Sharing the Summit of Everest

When I finally reached the last hump on the summit ridge
of Everest for the first time, I could see the three-legged aluminum survey pole put up by the Chinese. It twinkled a little
in the sun, but even so was difficult to make out properly.
Now I recognized the last part of the climb, the last 20 meters
to the summit. I could remember seeing pictures just like
this; I was absolutely sure now that there were but a few steps
to the summit. Even so, I did not trust myself to think that in
a few moments I would be standing on the roof of the world.
It was too overwhelming.

I waited two meters below the summit to let Ang Phu
catch up. Just before we stepped up onto the top, I took some
pictures—the highest point was exactly at eye-level, and it
was this short stretch of ridge that I photographed. Then I
put my arm round Ang Phu's shoulders and said to him: "We
must go up together." For me it was the happiest moment of
the expedition when we both stepped onto the summit. We
hugged each other and suddenly, like a little child, I began to
cry. I could see Ang Phu's face for he had taken off his mask,
as I then did also, and we could see our emotions mirrored in
the face of the other. It was not necessary to say much;

indeed, it was not necessary to say anything, only to look into our faces. Ang Phu murmured to himself gently and prayed. He prayed for us, for himself, and for everyone in the world.

At that moment I believe he was the happiest Nepali alive, the happiest Sherpa, for his Gods had suffered him to enter their kingdom, and he knew he was welcome there.

Music of the Mountain

The tripod just behind me was humming gently in the wind, yet I heard nothing except the music that had seemed to accompany me throughout my climb. It was a very rhythmic music, baroque music. I have tried to recapture the melody since, but it is impossible—the theme has gone forever. I heard this music on the summit, softly accompanied by vibrations in the air. There was nothing else to hear except the light wind, just this singing in my ears which doubtless had something to do with the pulsing of the blood, but it did not seem like that to me. It seemed to be the vibrations of the mountain I was experiencing.

The Last Few Steps

As I anticipate reaching the summit, I dare not look ahead any more for I don't want to know how far there is still to go. Some of the time I feel full of purpose and self-control in the face of the storm; but at other moments, I am filled with despair and try desperately to clench my teeth despite my wide-open, gasping mouth. Breathing becomes such a strenuous business that I scarcely have strength left to go on. Every 10 or 15 steps I collapse into the snow to rest, then crawl on again. My mind seems to have ceased to function. I simply go on climbing automatically. The fact that I am on Everest, the highest mountain in the world, is forgotten— nor does it register that I am climbing without oxygen apparatus.

The Very Top

The only thing that lures me on is that little point ahead,

where all the lines come together, the apex, the ultimate. The exertion now must be terrible, and yet I am insensible to it. It is as if the cortex of my brain were numb, as if only deeper inside my head there is something or somebody making decisions for me. I don't want to go on. I crawl, I cough, but I am drawn toward this farthest point, as if it were some magnetic pole, perhaps because to be there offers the only resolution. My mind is disconnected, dead. But my soul is alive and receptive, grown huge and palpable. It wants to reach the very top so that it can swing back into equilibrium.

Reaching the Top

The last few meters up to the summit no longer seem so hard. On reaching the top, I sit down and let my legs dangle into space. I don't have to climb anymore. Now, after the hours of torment, which indeed I didn't recognize as torment, now, when the monotonous motion of plodding upwards is at an end, and I have nothing more to do than breathe, a great peace floods my whole being. I breathe like someone who has run the race of his life and knows that he may now rest forever. I keep looking all around, because the first time I reached the summit of Everest I didn't see anything of the panorama I had expected, neither indeed did I notice how the wind was continually chasing snow across the summit.

In my state of spiritual abstraction, I no longer belong to myself and to my eyesight. I am nothing more than a single, narrow, gasping lung, floating over the mists and the summits. Only after I have drawn a couple of deep breaths do I again sense my legs, my arms, my head. I am in a state of bright, clear consciousness, even if not fully aware of where I am.

The summit seemed suddenly to me to be a refuge, and I had not expected to find any refuge up here. Looking at the steep, sharp ridges below, I have the impression that to have come later would have been too late.

An Eruption of Feeling

I am immediately shaken with sobs. I can neither talk nor think, feeling only how this momentous experience changes everything. To reach only a few meters below the summit would have required the same effort, the same anxiety and burden of sorrow, but a feeling like this, an eruption of feeling, is only possible on the summit. Everything that is, everything I am, is now colored by the fact that I have reached this special place. The summit—for the time being at least—is the simple intuitive answer to the enigma of life. There is no sense of triumph, no feeling of potency, only of being, and of thankfulness towards my partner. Everything else is forgotten in a wave of happiness. For a short while all reason is lost, and emotion holds sway; my feelings have taken over.

Summit Aftermath

I want only to rest a while, forget everything. At first there is no relief. I am leached, completely empty. In this emptiness, nevertheless, something like energy accumulates. I am charging myself up. For many hours I have only used up energy. I have climbed myself to a standstill; now I am experiencing regeneration, a return flow of energy. At the moment I am not at all disappointed that once again I have no view. I am standing on the highest point on earth for the second time, and again I can see nothing. I still don't know how I have made it, but I know that I can't do any more. In my tiredness I am not only as heavy as a corpse, I am incapable of taking anything in. I cannot distinguish above and below.

I Am the Summit

The energy which I derived from climbing and the stimulus of reaching the summit now fail me. I lie in the tent as if dead. Only the success keeps me alive. I obey the law of inertia. Between waking and sleeping, surrounded by the living dead, the hours slip away. I have no feeling of sublimity. I am too tired for that. And although I don't at this moment feel particularly special or happy, I have a hunch that in retrospect it will be comforting, a sort of conclusion. Perhaps a recognition that I too, like Sisyphus, shall have to roll that mythical stone all my life without ever reaching the summit; perhaps I myself am this summit. **MM**

*　*　*

Application and Action:

Application: We plan and prepare and push so hard to reach our career summits—in strategy, design, engineering, management, or sales—all for a few fleeting moments of gain and glory. What makes the summit more meaningful is Messner's ability to memorialize it and share it and assign meaning to it—so that it becomes much more than the conquering of the useless; rather, it becomes a timeless victory of human spirit and imagination over inert mass and internal emotions.

Action: Determine how you will make your summit quest and acquisition more meaningful for yourself and your team. **AA**

Chapter 9
Real Success

We are often fooled into seeking rather counterfeit imitations of success in the pursuit of possessions, positions, and public praise but the real prize in Messner's book is to experience being one with the world—a feeling of outer harmony and inner integrity, a gratitude for having survived so many ascents and descents, takeoffs and landings, mini-lives and near-deaths. Messner perhaps because he lives at the edge between success and failure is in a better position to define success and tell us what really matters most.

* * *

Physical Limits: Life and Death

To experience this feeling of oneness with the world, I must go to the limits of my physical ability. To climb a difficult face, at great height, I must exert the greatest physical expenditure and exhaustion. My worst enemy on the way to this goal of climbing a difficult face at great height is fear. I am a timid person, and like all timid people I long to overcome my fears. Victory over fear is also a form of happiness in which I am close to myself. Three times I set off alone for Nanga Parbat, and three times I turned back out of fear, before I had the power to overcome my fear and climb to the summit. I want to have the feeling of being stronger than my fear. That is why, again and again, I place myself in situations in which I meet fear in order to overcome it. But while I am attempting to resolve my isolation through experiences at the limit of my ability and to become master of my fears, I live. I live with an intensity which I can find nowhere else. And so every descent from the mountain is for me less a return to life and much more a descent from a piece of life lived to the fullest—a small death.

Success and Failure

Success isn't more useful than failure on the frontier. It just releases different feelings. Night plunges everything into uncertainty. Self-doubts belong to humans, and doubts energize us to ask the question of what it all means. A person whose ambition becomes eagerness is no longer a player. My frontier crossings are tests of ideas (theories, inventions, abilities) in relation to experience. My way is based on trial and removal of error. The illusion of safety paralyzes the spirit of life. Nevertheless, explorers are not fascinated by danger as prisoners are of liberty. I am neither a combat machine nor a fitness miracle. I'm also no fanatic of stamina. I am much more vulnerable and more limited than people believe. I seek a new course with highest value of experience against failure.

Success is difficult to measure. I can fail and yet be successful in getting ahead in life. Failure throws us back to a human standard again and again. He who fails modifies that which he can modify; he assumes the unalterable and develops wisdom to differentiate the changeable from the unchangeable. Making and correcting mistakes promotes the power of innovation.

Not knowing beforehand where I shall land doesn't make my existence more meaningful—but it makes it more intensive. No more knowing the ins and outs at the starting point of a new, creative idea. I comprehend limitations as opportunities. I hope to continue living a few more years by breaking away—staying free for more beautiful things. So much is learned by failing and by breaking away. Long-term success is only possible when failure is also allowed.

Success as Rising Again

I can have success in the long run only if I may fail. How can I play without losing, without failing? If success should come through time due to my ability, good luck, or coincidence, losing would be involved, whether it be sooner or later. The result would be too great of a distance from reality. And loss of reality invariably leads sooner or later to conclusive failure. We all are humans, and as such, we are limited. We all make mistakes. Because of this we must all learn to tolerate the failure of others.

I understand failure as a repeated chance. I have often come out of failure with new determination and clearer conceptions. To ascend all 14 of the 8,000-meter peaks I took 30 expeditions: 18 times I got to the summit; 12 times I failed.

The only reason I reached my goal in the end was because I rose when I fell. I never gave up. To advance further than others, I must be able to get up more often than others. I must learn to bear frequent failure. Inferiority makes one modest, wise, and tolerant.

The successful person is more often ready to begin anew than are all others who fail. We must not allow joy to perish when we descend. To retrieve experiences from failure and to try to go beyond the previous point of return is worthwhile in every case.

My life goal does not consist of accumulating as many successes as possible. I am naturally pleased with successes. Success also makes one self-confident, strong, successful. Nothing is more successful than success itself.

Success as a Habit

What is there to be discovered is not the mountain, but the person. There is a grand experience hidden in a successful expedition that helps me build a positive self-image. This is transferrable to all areas of life. I perceive every successful act as a distinction which I give myself: self-respect grows and has stability, even if it is not eternal. Giving up repeatedly weakens a person. A reached goal becomes a type of habit.

Success as Moving Beyond Appearances

Vision and image are happily not the same thing. Personality and image are seldom the same. Enduring success is achieved only when a person identifies with his facts and not with his image. It was not raw strength that brought me so far. Not even "risk joy." Perhaps it was selecting the right partners and trying to be the right partner.

How faithful we stay when third parties or outsiders have taken away our self-understanding is reflected in our successes. Even border-crossers often get "burned out" before they have reached the zenith of their performance. Or they run behind short-lived fashion trends. How to distinguish between reality and appearance, if the interested person does not perceive it himself? Only a factual relationship sharpens the view of what is valid, real, enduring. The only thing that counts is what is, and not what one would like it to be.

Although I produce nothing more with my border-crossings than experiences, I am like an enterprise: full of ideas, planning, and productivity. I am an idea-man industrialist.

Success as Overcoming Opposition

The retroactive giving of meaning is a typical consequence of real success. At the start, there exists an idea; then there are detours, setbacks, opposition, experiments, and risks. Only through tests, accidents, and persistence does the "one right solution" come out—and future success become clear.

Success as Keeping Hope Alive

Anyone who has not experienced this life in wetness, humidity, and darkness cannot imagine it. Everything, including all noise, is lost in the expanse. I cannot classify anything here—not the silence, not the smells, and not the accumulated expanses, which, like concentrations of darkness, never pretend to be nothingness. The world still must be created here. We travel through this disordered world. And only because we have so many practical problems, we walk without becoming conscious of the hopelessness which radiates this massive uniformity. As we lose our view in the fog, certainties lose themselves. We know all and nothing about our position. If hope is lost in the unknown, a puzzle cannot even emerge to the front or to the rear. Nothing is left for us to do but wait. The role of the leader is to keep hope alive.

Success as Meeting Goals

With success on Makalu in the autumn of 1986, and a permit in my pocket to attempt Lhotse immediately afterward, I knew that at long last I stood a chance of realizing my goal—one of my goals, that is. I would probably have to forgo climbing one of the 8,000ers in winter. If I did manage to climb Lhotse, and thereby complete ascents of all 14 of the world's highest mountains, I wanted to keep the promise I had made to my mother, not to embark on any more expeditions to the 8,000ers, at least with the intention of going to the top myself.

I have done almost everything there is to do on the 8,000ers. I have been on big expeditions, small expeditions, and made solo ascents; I have climbed in spring, summer and autumn; I have climbed these mountains by easy ways and by the most difficult routes; I have traversed them; I have climbed them with various partners, but I have never reached the top of one in winter. I have had to turn back often enough to have learned how to lose without giving up. This has saved my life.

There was no sense of heroism or conquest after climbing all 14 of the 8,000ers, merely the satisfaction of having realized a complex idea, a target I had set myself. The obligation to climb all 8,000ers without bottled oxygen and in as fair a style as possible was something I had assumed voluntarily. No one had set the rules or conditions for me in advance, apart from Mother Nature. Because, to a certain extent, I had fulfilled the obligation, I was pleased with myself, at least in this respect.

All the same, I know that not only is it a tragedy *not* to achieve one's goal, it is perhaps an even greater tragedy to do so.

Success as Moving On

For the time being, I have no worries about my future. There are plenty of new ideas, new goals. The 8,000ers are ingrained deeply in the mind of the public, but they don't interest me that much. Not just Alpinists, but millions of ordinary people are beginning to take the 8,000ers seriously, at a time when they should no longer be taken so seriously. Now, because I have survived ascents of all 14 mountains, this realization has outlived its importance—at least, it has for me. This kind of adventure has become outmoded. It is now an institution, and by assuming a mundaneness has become antiquated.   **MM**

* * *

Application and Action:

Application: The message here is to move beyond appearances and superficial substitutes and seek the real success that comes from facing yourself, overcoming barriers, and building as a natural consequence of meaningful action a positive self-image and healthy self-respect. Messner's view of success—as overcoming fear, keeping hope alive, meeting goals, and then moving on—shows us a path toward a fulfilling future.

Action: Imagine what "real success" would look like for you and your team, and then take the path that leads to it.   **AA**

Solo on Mount Everest

*by Chris Bonington, expedition leader and
Mount Everest Climber*

Reinhold Messner's unique success in his mountaineering career is epitomized in what is probably his finest achievement—his solo ascent of Everest. He combines a mixture of pioneering boldness, tackling the seemingly impossible, with a sound realism that enables him to analyze the many factors for any particular project and then overcome them in an effective way.

We can see this in Reinhold's approach to Everest. The concept of climbing the highest mountain on earth, solo, in a single push was so colossal that he needed to approach it in a series of creative stages. His ascent with Peter Habeler, without oxygen, by the South Col route—in itself a huge step into the unknown—was a necessary step also in ascertaining that the human body could attain the height of 29,028 feet without the aid of oxygen.

He also needed to acclimatize himself to the loneliness of the Himalayan giants. In this respect, his solo ascent of Nanga Parbat gave him the reassurance that he could cope with the immense mental and physical stress of facing a Himalayan peak on his own. In bringing together his experience on Everest without oxygen and his self-reliance on Nanga Parbat, he could then realistically face what must have been his ultimate challenge. The very speed, sureness, and efficiently of this ascent of the world's highest mountain masks the size of the barrier he was breaking.

Section III

* * *

Challenges

Between us and our stretch goals stand many obstacles and challenges, perhaps even a few mountains. In this section, Messner dissects these inner and outer barriers to success as no man can without first passing through the gauntlet of highs and lows, hot and cold, heaven and hell, fire and ice, fear and faith. He addresses fear as a friend, as a signal of life and a warning of impending death. Having paid the price of success, he informs us what each coin is worth in a realm where there is opposition to all good things.

Chapter 10
Inner and Outer Barriers

What lies between us and our goals? Besides the obvious outer barriers—including the formidable mountain itself—we face the inner demons of doubt, fears, and false hopes. Messner cautions us against trying to "fake it until you make it" for the sake of maintaining an image. He suggests that nothing false will hold up well on the face (of the mountain). For those of us who are prepared, climbing the face provides relief from nagging doubts and helps us focus on the positive side of performance and progress.

*   *   *

16 Years of Worries, Doubts, and Fears

Today, when I look back over my 16 Himalayan years, I remember those moments when I wanted to give it all up, when the very thought of climbing a 8,000-meter mountain terrified me. I was prey to all manner of doubts and fears. How often I questioned whether I should go on or not. Those 16 years in the Himalayas represents 16 long years of training and sweating, worrying and wondering. To abide by the discipline of risk—which you must to assure survival—demands concentration and endurance. Sixteen years of repeated failure and fresh starts—that was my key to success.

Hopeless Situations

In what appear to be hopeless situations, like my retreat from winter in Greenland, severe doubt develops. Soon you begin to doubt everything and everybody. You have doubts about the meaning of such a venture, doubt about your own ability, doubt about life itself. But if you endure this doubt well, you are rewarded with new ideas, fresh beliefs, clear insights, and real solutions.

Facing My Fears

I don't climb mountains simply to vanquish their summits. What would be the point of that? I place myself voluntarily into dangerous situations to learn to face my own fears and doubts, my innermost feelings. Anyone who lets himself be confronted with an extreme goal is full of fears. During the course of my life, I have even become more fearful. Also because with each experience, I know more what dangerous, unforeseeable, and impossible things can happen to me. Mostly, these fears are unjustified. For it is the fear of fear that bothers us—especially fear of starting out—that presents to all of us the possibility of failure, including death. For me, fear is a regulator for what I should do.

Fear Has Its Place

Fear belongs to adventure just as does risk. It is a signal for a concrete threat. The more sensitive I am to it, the better I can guard against, avoid, and encounter dangers. I have never smiled at the fears of others, nor have I ever had problems acknowledging fear as a part of my feelings. Naturally it is easy to upbraid myself to master these fears and not to be ruled by them. But to completely switch off, to eliminate all negative thoughts, is so difficult! To let myself go—and at the same time be as alert as a cat—is a trait that belongs to me, just like my hands, my eyes and this horizon of glass, which has stamped my life more than anything else. Fear is like a clenched fist. Only an open hand needs no energy. At present I lack the inner harmony to dispel all fear and be like an open hand. I need so much emotional strength to thrust aside all the possible dangers of a solo ascent of Everest which fill my mind. Only when the stream of these fears dries up can I set out!

Natural Doubts

Naturally all this worry, doubt, and aggression has its effect on me. My enthusiasm is dampened a bit. All the same I still want to try it, go for it, against all premonition. Swimming against the tide raises doubts, but at the same time, I find that the constant battle with the many outside critics and obstacles serves in a way to strengthen my resolve—not only so far as mountains are concerned, but in the rest of my life, too. It is not just out of stubbornness that I want to prove to my critics that I am right: I want to test my conviction that it is possible to climb Everest alone without bottled oxygen.

Inner Barriers

The real hurdles on these very big mountains are often not to be found on the face itself, but come from within ourselves: feelings of isolation and apprehension, and frequent waves of doubt and dizziness, all of which I experienced with particular acuteness at the foot of Annapurna. These negative feelings and emotions are what so often rob me of my enthusiasm for a climb, my courage, and with it, my strength. It's in the grey light of dawn, or at the foot of a big wall, and sometimes, too, during the organization and preparation for a tour, that worries and doubts present such an inhibiting barrier.

Fear as a Companion

Fear is a constant companion. You can't live life fully without it. When things get critical, your fear becomes even more intense. But when I climb, I do so with hardly any doubts or worries. I make the decision about what I can or cannot do as I go along, step by step and day by day. Fear is a an essential element in this quest, and I pay attention to it. It's natural. If you remain conscious that death is part of life, you cannot suppress your basic fear of falling, of being over-whelmed by the weather, or overrun by an avalanche.

Self-Doubt

On the way back from Kangchenjunga, I reproached myself bitterly for the way things had turned out. Worn out from the wind, cold and exertion, I was full of self-doubt. I could no longer see any sense in such expeditions. I don't think it was so much tiredness and resignation that dampened my enthusiasm for our enterprise as it was my illness. Above all, it was having to see how my companions suffered. During the climb I had never inquired of myself whether it made sense or nonsense: during the period of effort, on this as other climbs, I was my own answer. But in the state of mind I was in afterward, I wanted to abandon the rest of the expedition. What did it really mean to climb three 8,000-meter moun-tains in one season? Kangchenjunga had only been the start of a grand idea; setting out for Gasherbrum II and Broad Peak within the ensuing months would perhaps propel me into even worse hardships. Only the knowledge that we had come through by the skin of our teeth, enabled me to hold up my head. I was a man.

Price of Success

I have paid for my success dearly. Old friends suddenly regarded me with suspicion. I had become too famous for them, no longer belonged to them as I did before. Because of my publicity and exposure in the media, they felt "betrayed." In the many interviews and discussions that were prompted by the criticism we received, I defended my style of expedi-tion as a wonderful opportunity for mountaineering. A thou-sand times I answered several questions taking me to task over this or that. Becoming better known gave me better chances of financing my expeditions; but it left me with less time than before—less time for new ideas, and less time for my friends. People believed I had become self-important and aloof, when exactly the opposite was the case. It is true I was possessed with a desire to do more; but my needs for acceptance by friends and for an exchange of ideas were greater than ever. **MM**

* * *

Application and Action:

Application: What do you gain by facing your fears and embracing your doubts? Messner's answer is convincing: you gain a friend, a trusted advisor who may save your life if you abide by the discipline of risk as a regulator of what you should do in any instance, especially in those "hopeless" situations when all is seemingly lost.

Action: Assess the inner and outer barriers that stand in the way of your summit—between where you are today and where you hope to be tomorrow. Face them in the light of day when you have a much better chance of overcoming them. **AA**

Chapter 11

Criticism

Perhaps nothing can stop us in our tracks faster than an avalanche of criticism. When people are second guessing all that goes wrong and criticizing and castigating the leaders, we are caught in the crossfire. But what hurts most is criticism from within—from colleagues and friends and self. Withstanding unjust criticism, whatever its source, is the tough test of those who aspire to crossing borders and breaking new ground. Real innovation of any kind seems to invite scrutiny and reproach. And so the innovative leader needs a thick skin and a brave heart.

* * *

Reproached by Critics

It used to be sacrilege for amateurs, as well as experienced climbers, to climb through the most difficult routes in the Alps alone. I was stamped as "crazy," as a "suicide." I did it anyway. Smiling, I heard the many reproaches from "mature" people, those who saw life through the television, those who stopped scoffing at my "craziness" only after I could no longer get excited for this form of exploration.

Criticism for Tragedy

When I returned home from climbing Manaslu in 1972, I read the first of many articles criticizing our expedition, articles written by people who had never themselves climbed 8,000 meters and were unlikely ever to do so. What could they know about what it means to climb at such great heights? To stay alive in hurricane winds of 100km an hour? To fall over in the snow 30 times? To not believe in yourself any more? What it's like to have no strength left at all; to repeatedly pull yourself together, get back on to your feet, and go on searching? What it's like to search in a storm for a tent, a little space of two square meters where under its protective awning I might survive the night?

Many people not only blame me for the tragedies and deaths that have occurred on our expeditions, they have been vitriolic in their condemnation. It has been very wounding, but I have not given in to it. I have stood accused of "treading over the bodies" of my companions. But when I was going for the summit of Manaslu, there was not the remotest intimation of possible tragedy. The weather conditions were good; Franz Jager was in fine shape when he left me. It was only when I was coming back down that the storm suddenly broke; and it was in that moment, just as suddenly, that tragedy befell us.

Criticism Before and After

When word came out that I wanted to climb Everest without oxygen, there was even more opposition to me and my ideas than ever before. Pundits appeared on television, at great press conferences, saying that we might reach the summit of Everest without oxygen masks, but we certainly would not make it back down again. And if we did, we would be mental vegetables.

And then after our success, I was criticized as never before because of my "risk joy," my "wearing partners out" and my "egomania." My image became that of a madman. What should I do? It is impossible for me always to be doing something "correct," "reasonable," and "useful." There should be no disgrace in doing something "false," or "crazy" when everyone else is doing something "correct," or "reasonable."

Maybe this is backwards. The world has become crazy in the meantime—what is "normal" is outside the limits.

Talk Is Cheap

That we should find the Dhaulagiri South Face impossible to climb was something that many of our fans, sponsors and even the cameramen who were making a film of the attempt refused to accept. That gave the critics something to get their teeth into. People who themselves had never climbed an 8,000er, knew exactly how it should be done. Others claimed equally to know that it was madness from the start. Down on the flat, talk is easy.

It's always like that with us. Not only outsiders, but observing cameramen and even expedition members think differently in the security of Base Camp than they do on the face. Back home, often they can't understand how we could have "run away" in the face of danger.

Criticism as Affirmation

The massive criticism in connection with my Antarctic expedition might also be understood as an answer to my self-motivation and an affirmation of my motivation to do this for every "desk worker" who spends his or her time either in the office or at home, but would much rather be traveling on the "eternal ice." Since they did not perceive either a sprouting self-criticism or a need to change their lives, they had to react to me with aggression. Not because I provoked them by my actions. Because I always place my life in question, I also put their lives into question.

Withstanding Criticism

Only the strong withstand injustice. Although border-crossings—especially those that lie just at the edge of what is possible—have been equated with leisure time, we border-crossers face many prejudices and opposition. I had found a way to make climbing my career in my life. I can therefore go my way quite peacefully. If, however, anyone wants to characterize this deviation from a prescribed professional career as a dropout mentality, I would answer him, "I'm glad to be a drop-out, because I refuse to condemn myself to one-dimensionality." Anyone who admires something other than traditional work and loves it like a game is not thereby a work-destroyer.   **MM**

*   *   *

Application and Action:

Application: Consider what positive or constructive uses you might make of the criticism you receive. For example, from thoughtful and responsible criticism, you might discover blind spots, learn what might be improved, or take an extra step to prevent problems next time. Of course, if the criticism stems from prejudice, aggression or jealousy, you may just have to find a way to endure it.

Action: Develop the capacity for turning criticism into an affirmation or a source of positive change, growth, and improvement.   **AA**

Chapter 12
Risk and Danger

When risk is real and danger high, the challenge becomes one of moment-to-moment risk management, seeking the right balance between risk and reward, danger and delivery. In this chapter, Messner explains why he is still alive today to tell of his adventures: he stops when the control of risk runs out. He suggests that anyone with a "life wish" responsibly assumes calculated risk and avoids exposing himself to unnecessary dangers. Even when you sense danger on all sides, you may escape death by playing the best option and knowing the odds. And yes, "lady luck" may be your only saving grace when lightening strikes.

* * *

Risks and Rewards

Toward the end of the Dhaulagiri South Face expedition, Otto Wiedemann, then a German military climbing instructor and the youngest man in our team, was scared to death of the face and its terrifying avalanches—not without reason. But no sooner had he flown home, than it seemed to him he had been too weak. He was asking himself if he had pushed "the attack" hard enough, wondering if he had put enough into the climb, and sensing he had not risked enough. In big mountaineering, striking the exact balance between the commitment required to bring about a successful outcome and needless self-sacrifice is a fine art. If I am still alive today, it is

111

not because I am a bolder climber, but rather that I am a fearful one who seeks the perfect balance between risk and reward.

Risk Management

Mountaineering is capable of expression through the management of risk. The bigger the risk, the more difficult it is to do what is right—and what is right is that which permits us to survive. Coming home safely is all that matters. So here again, the question becomes: Have the possibilities—the products of mountain, experience, equipment, know-how—become so great that we are running blindly into a trap? Are we too human with our longings and our ambition?

Climbing, which arises out of ideas and big mountains, develops an individual dynamic. It is only justifiable when we stop where the control of risk runs out. Someone who exposes himself to dangers that cannot be avoided is either a fool or afflicted with a death wish—he is certainly not a climber aware of his responsibilities. That is something I have always striven to be—a responsible, sensible climber who manages risk superbly well. I have striven harder for this goal than for all the summits of this world.

Risk Is Resistance

Risk generally belongs to an intensive life. An artist, an athlete, a businessperson accepts risks in his or her sphere. Risks grow on people. Risk is the resistance which we detect, assume, wish to master—or the resistance we choose to go around. The person who better masters risk management will also be more successful. The risk involved in climbing a vertical cliff is somewhat different than the risk encountered in a business enterprise. The person who climbs solo and falls is dead. A manager who makes a substantial error "only" buries his company in sand. I do not wish to mystify the risk on the mountain, however. I accept it. It belongs to the act. Thus I am not fascinated or hypnotized by risk. I do not look for it, but I learn to live with the reality. Likewise, life is risk. More intensity means more risk. But I am not too frightened by it, because I allow myself "failure." The termination of an expedition, the so-called failure, is not a fault or a loss, but an important learning experience—a vital step in the growth process.

Calculated Risk

I was well aware of the risk involved in turning our attentions to Dhaulagiri immediately after coming off Annapurna. Trying to climb two 8,000ers in such quick succession would not only be very draining, it would place a great strain on luck. Everyone has luck, but only up to a point. Once your allotment of luck is spent, a climb becomes dangerous—and it may no longer be possible to mobilize those reserves that are so vital in an emergency. Perhaps we would find ourselves too tired to carry through such a climb. I confess that in moments of real danger, something acts inside me as a defense mechanism; it aids survival. But as soon as the threat is past, it evaporates in thin air.

Survival as a Measure of Success

Luckily, climbing is not capable of being expressed in terms of records or numbers. It certainly cannot be measured in seconds, meters of height, or grades. Survival is the most meaningful measure. I was lucky. The Gods were kind to me. I wish the same to all others who are enthralled by the 8,000ers. Luck is a component that accompanies great risk. We all need luck, for the mountains are infinitely bigger than us. Mere men can never "vanquish" them. "The Gods have won" the Tibetans say whenever they venture up a mountain or a high pass. And I say it too. I am not so proud of having climbed all 14 of the 8,000-meter mountains in the world. I do not regard it as much. I am not proud of the "success," although I sought it for a long time. I am proud to have survived. A border-crosser—in hiking, ice-crossing, mountain-climbing, and desert-crossing—is one who neither fights nor conquers nature. He also does not want to dominate it. As part of a simultaneously chaotic and ordered whole, he reacts only in such a way that he does not upset the balance, even at the limits of the possible (danger, effort, fear). I too want to survive; but not in an arm chair in front of the television, but in the most difficult situations. Only one who has a fine and multiple sense for the outer and inner world will have success in the wilderness and survive.

Safety Comes from Within

Safety on a large expedition is often only an illusion. A mountain that is surrounded by six camps—usually with some Alpinists and bearers in each—is surely "secured" in case of a catastrophe (storm, avalanche, earthquake), but not any safer. In fact, the risks of death are even greater. A small group is stronger as a summit team or the foundation of a great expedition. The individual mountain-climbers on a small expedition run greater risks than do individuals on a large expedition. The total number of risks is much higher, however, on the large expedition. It is unreasonable to make a border-crossing safe two, three, and four times over, because the total risks are increased thereby. I believe that protection in a border-crossing is often equivalent to compensating for a lack of safety. Border-crossers without risk are no longer border-crossers!

Safety can only come from within, from out of our self-understanding, which is based, in part, on ability, experience, and endurance. All protection is worth nothing if the basic conditions and wise instincts are lacking. Self-assurance is the basis of all safety. Protection is involved sporadically, as a life-saving measure, as a saving anchor in the case of unforeseen events, weaknesses, and collapses.

Adventure is not possible with total redundancy. If I bring all technical achievements, all modern possibilities for protection into the game, neither abandonment nor impossibilities are conceivable. Both are part of border-crossings. Without them, there is no risk, nor readiness for risk. I have always been curious, always kept a look-out for new paths, and strived to expand my limits—in mountain-climbing and in my personal life—farther outward, feeling that this was the best path to real safety and security.

Speed Is Safety

Some people believe that slower is safer. But I believe that a border crossing driven to the top is fairer, cleaner, faster, and in some ways also safer. Speed is also safety. There is no loss of time through joint decision making. In storms, illnesses or mistakes, a correction or a deviation is problematic, if not impossible, with a slow, large group. As the climber's speed increases, the danger in dangerous natural zones like Nanga Parbat decreases, but it is never eliminated. With my solo hikes (featuring new, dangerous routes, essentially no technological aids, no preparatory work), I come closest to my ideal of a futuristic border crossing of a mountain because the danger is greater than the difficulty.

Moving Mountains

What I do is only seemingly more dangerous than what a dedicated business manager does. Just as some people from my age group and my circle of acquaintances have fallen to their deaths or frozen, many others have died of a heart attack or in a car accident. It seems paradoxical that mountain-climbing—driven by calculated risks—is not more dangerous that any other intensive activity. Every profession has its particular health and safety risks. Everyone risks his life in his field in his own way. Now, a possible heart attack is not as visible as a possible 3,000-meter fall to death. And this is my advantage. I am confronted directly by my dangers. But if I walk through the city, I do not see the roof tile that might fall on my head. I also don't see all the great social and environmental threats that bump up against humanity. The outrages in our world, in spite of better knowledge, are committed in groups and always by people. In the face of global dangers, we happily stick our heads in the sand and play games. We are endangered like no other people has ever been endangered. The possible environmental catastrophes that may strike us are more deadly than rock slides and avalanches. Not for one person, but for millions, even billions of people. Making this danger known is a task; to eliminate it globally is our duty. These are the great "mountains" that have to be moved.

Minimizing Danger

Climbing could not exist without danger. Without risk there would be no adventure. That, I believe, it what gives mountaineering its worth. The fool is not the person who goes up there in full knowledge that climbing is hazardous, but the one who does not want to know about death, who shuts his eyes to the fact that even he could be killed. Each of the 14 8,000ers can be a serious undertaking if conditions are bad. When a storm blows in, if the climber has insufficient strength to get himself down quickly, he can soon find himself in a desperate position. Every 8,000er can be fatal if we are not careful, or if we run out of luck. For example, a glacier may be relatively quiet, and yet we are naturally aware of how much risk still remains. By choosing the best time of day, we expose ourselves to less danger and for a shorter time, but immense danger still exists.

Danger on All Sides

In descending through a very steep passage between the seracs, we feel threatened from all sides. The danger does not need spelling out—we could sense the danger virtually throughout our whole bodies, especially in our backs, as we climbed down past these ice towers. They could have collapsed at any moment. Only when we were right down to the bottom, when we had raced clear of the steep face out into the Gasherbrum Valley, did we allow ourselves to feel any sort of jubilation. We had escaped death! We could breathe freely. A safe distance from the face, we sat down on our rucksacks to rest. Several times we looked up, retracting our descent route in our minds. That we had just climbed down this icefall was unbelievable, even to us.

Odds of Success

The chances of success are always narrow, and just because we were prepared to push it to the "limits of the impossible," we were not some kind of suicide squad. "Death of Glory" was not our motto. On Dhaulagiri, we were not climbing for the public, not for television or for any other institution. We were not climbing for our country nor any Alpine organization, but just for ourselves. When, via the press and television, we accepted a transient and widely scattered audience, it did not mean that we agreed to play the heroes. We were not prepared to heroically sacrifice ourselves. I never have been willing to feed the mass media with the usual clichés about climbing— calling it a contempt of death, recklessness, or playing with lives. Perhaps some time I will go back to the South Face of Dhaulagiri, but not out of any heroic or glorious gesture, rather out of curiosity. Should I go again, however, it will be with the same principles regarding risk discipline as on the first occasion. If I had any wish to kill myself, I know simpler methods and less beautiful places.

Lightening Strikes

The fact that we were not struck by lightning on the summit of Dhaulagiri surprised even us. A few months afterwards when I was traveling in Tibet and learned that my brother Siegfried had been killed by lightning on a mountain, the fact of my survival seemed even more inexplicable, shocking even. It seemed so unfair that I should still be alive and he was dead. I am not suggesting that mountains like one person and not another. Mountains are neither wicked nor kind to us. They are nothing more than an organic mass. But to us, they appear unpredictable, and they are not fully understood scientifically. They have no will of their own, no emotions.

They do not draw us to them, but equally they do not shake us off. They represent for us a marvelous opportunity to gain meaningful experience. And because they are infinitely bigger than we are, they remain a dangerous medium at all levels. By comparison to the mountains, we are tiny. Our instincts are ill-developed, our endurance quickly runs out, and our strength is limited. Big mountains will always remain a useful medium for us to test ourselves.

In Tibet in 1985, this land where death belongs to life, when I learned that Siegfried was dead, I took the news quietly, accepting the irrationaly of it as somehow inevitable, although it still grieved me deeply. My mother, who had now lost two sons in the mountains, did not try and persuade me to give up climbing expeditions. She only asked me to promise to give up the 8,000ers if I were to climb all 14 of them, and not to do any more after that. So, in the knowledge that my mother understood, I kept going.

Aftermath of Danger

When the ordeal was over—when I reached the foot of the mountain and no longer had to worry about falling, dying of exhaustion, or freezing to death—I collapsed. I no longer had to grope forward in the midst; no longer summon my whole will to take another step forward—and with that, all will left me. As long as there was danger, I had been able to keep going up or coming down, but in the instant the danger was all behind me, I was finished, physically and emotionally spent.

Storm Danger

On Lhotse we ventured our summit climb in a storm, the like of which I had only previously endured coming off a mountain. On none of my earlier expeditions to 8,000ers would I have considered setting out for the summit in that sort of weather. I don't know why we risked more this time than before. I can only say that Hans and I felt safe making the climb. Only when we stood between the two summit horns of Lhotse did we hesitate a moment. There we could smell the danger, but the proximity of the summit strengthened our confidence. To go on meant the whole business could be concluded. On the summit this time there was no time for joy, only a deep anxiety to get back down. The descent, too, required our fullest concentration. Only the next day, when we had safely crossed the icefall and were nearing base camp, did a sort of elemental joy wash into me. Not so much, "Hurray! I've done it!," but rather the joy of being alive at all, coupled with the feeling that I was now free for other things. **MM**

* * *

Application and Action:

Application: What risks and dangers do you face and how are you managing risk to increase the odds of success in your venture? We learn from Messner to be wise and take only calculated risks that mitigate the extreme danger to be found in every tough test.

Action: Do your own risk assessment and evaluate the balance between risk and reward. Are you "pushing the attack" enough? Too much? Devise a wise risk management plan of action. **AA**

Chapter 13

Fatigue and Burnout

Fatigue can certainly make cowards of us all, turning work or "play" into a painful endurance test. Messner documents the conditions that lead to fatigue and burnout, the natural consequences of these dreadful conditions, and how to rise to the challenge. There's a fine line between success and failure, and often having the courage and faith to take just one more step toward the goal is enough to cross over the line and save the day. To recover from burnout, Messner allows himself a few breaks and rest stops. And after an ordeal or failure, he may take a season to recover and reinvent himself for the next great climb of his career.

* * *

Physical and Mental Fatigue

How much easier is the descent of a great mountain! It takes only a fraction of the effort, will-power, and stamina compared with coming up. And yet not only during the ascent but also during the descent my will-power is often dulled. The longer I climb, the less important the goal seems to me, the more indifferent I become to my goal. My attention is diminished, and my memory is weakened. My mental fatigue is now as great or greater than my bodily fatigue. It is so pleasant to sit doing nothing—but, therefore, so dangerous. Death through exhaustion is—like death through freezing—a pleasant one.

An Endurance Test

As I traverse the undulating ridge above the North Col I feel as if I am returning from a shadow world. I make myself carry on through my tiredness, using the knowledge that I have been on the summit. I offer no more resistance, but let myself fall at each step. Only I may not remain sitting. Day after day I endured the loneliness of the undulating snow surface of the North Face; hour after hour I walked against the wind, feeling the sharp ice grains that swirl with it; for an eternity I meandered through the mist, which deluded me into thinking each block of rock was a friend. Each breath I took up there was an ordeal, and still I took it as a gift because it gave me another day of life.

Burnout and Exhaustion

The physical and spiritual conditions of exhaustion and burnout leave behind loss of desire, and often even loss of hope. How can a formerly engaged person orient himself anew, when even his own ideals seem stale or empty because they themselves are burned out? Such a person first needs enough time to start over—relaxation, friends, new daydreams—and second, he or she needs a new playing field that corresponds to him or her. This person first needs to come out of the "inner emigration," and then create hope with other means. Fine-tuned people often develop instincts to feel earlier than others that they want to climb, or even that they should climb. One step from climbing burnout means to put more elan, more fundamental energy into life. To find the right moment for climbing is helpful, but it's difficult to learn. I think that I must climb before I am completely burned out. And I always need peace, relaxation, and reflection to be able to jump back in with both feet again.

Burnout Reduces Commitment

Getting burned out slowly rattles my whole person to a reduced commitment. The reality that I feel emptiness after every success, at least for a short time, has little to do with it. This emptiness cannot be equated with burnout. Burnout has a destructive power. It manifests itself through extreme loss of energy. A realized idea is simply an empty vision to me—something I had been excited about, engaged in, identified with—and then lost with the realization of it.

Both burnout and this type of emptiness after the realization of a vision have nothing to do with escaping. In youthful years, I would often flee from reality through my climbing excursions. In so doing, I had more of a feeling of escaping reality. Also, when I would change my focus from one thing to another, I would feel as if I were escaping during the transitions. I used to think I could climb my entire life, even alone, as long as I identified with it. In 1969, the most active climbing period of my life, as I dreamed of going one step further in the elegance and difficulty of first attempts, my interests abruptly changed. I didn't notice it at first, but I felt that I had to apply myself to another field—later it would be climbing the highest peaks—to rise above previous experiences. Everyone's abilities and possibilities are required in specific times of their lives.

One Step from Burnout

The "burnout syndrome" is not only familiar to social workers, business people and politicians, but also to adventurers. He who has lived near the limits of maximum stress for a space of time sooner or later feels fatigue, aversion, maybe even doubt about his own abilities. The doubt is less about purpose and more about himself. The result is a serious departure from efficiency, creativity, and motivation. In extreme cases, burnout leads to psychosomatic sicknesses, and sometimes even to fits of despair and apathy. Some say that explorers—who should have learned to react to conflicts—would quickly find their way out of the vicious circle of exhaustion: the circle in which the point of view continually narrows. It no longer works to simply tune things out, the "inner emigration" of the previous escape route remains. It is the other way around. Such people, those who often place excessive demands on themselves, are often sacrifices of burnout syndrome. When we turn back in extreme situations, we most efficiently defer being burned out.   **MM**

* * *

Application and Action:

Application: How do fatigue and burnout foil your business or personal pursuits? Messner shows how these conditions can kill commitment, sap energy, and lead to sickness, despair, and apathy. In your application, you might consider how best to battle fatigue and avoid deadly burnout in your business ventures.

Action: Guard against placing excessive demands on yourself and your team. Rather than make yourself a human sacrifice to the "burnout syndrome," find a way to escape and take your "game" to the next level.   **AA**

Chapter 14
Alone and Lonely—Solo

Not only might you be "lonely at the top," you may be alone along the way. Much of Messner's success can be attributed to his ability to be alone, climb alone, and cope with loneliness—perhaps the toughest of all challenges. In this chapter, Messner tells us why he often ventures out alone and what he discovers on his solo climbs about himself. He also shares his deep sense of loneliness, even the feeling of being "alone in a crowd," and the immense rewards that come from relying on your own resources. Of great interest is his account of how he compensates for the lack of companionship and security, how he overcomes the fear of being alone, and how he prepares himself for the solo experience.

✻   ✻   ✻

Why Solo?

Why did I climb Everest a second time? Who is paying me for it? Who is backing me? That's what people want to know. I was also asked which flag I had taken with me, for which country did I climb. I say that I do it for myself, on my own incentive, with my own means.

"I am my own homeland, and my handkerchief is my flag," I say, quoting a favorite belief.

"Why did you go completely alone?"

" I am always afraid of being alone."

"Was it only crazy record seeking?"

"Records arise out of the increase in technical and physical performances in known spheres. My solo climb was a thrust into the unknown—unknown not only on account of the weather conditions during the monsoon, unknown above all in respect of the boundless possibilities of the human body and spirit."

The Positive Side of Lonely

When you are alone, you notice how you love yourself. Solitude is the clearest mirror of self-love. The fact of loneliness is an essential problem of humanity. Loneliness is not negative or positive, however. It is part of being human, of living with values. Many of us fear being alone. Since the beginning of time, loneliness has concerned people. Loneliness and death are closely related to each other. Even though many of us do not want to accept this reality—to think and talk about it—I think positively about death, because I also receive loneliness positively.

The Rewards of Soloing

In 1980 when I made my solo ascent of Everest during the monsoon period, there was not another soul anywhere above base camp. For five whole days I climbed in complete isolation, dependent solely on my own resources—and putting myself further from the inhabited earth with every upward step. My body was a wreck at the end of it; I survived despite myself, but as a worn-out shell. By contrast, many of today's Everest "conquerors" are far better at managing their bodies than their minds. The preoccupation for this "no-limits" generation is a quick thrill, rather than choosing the toilsome solitary path with its lengthy periods of sorrow and anguish. They race up prepared trails, ill acclimatized as often as not, from one established camp to the next. Without giving much thought to what they do, they follow a trend, an ideology that glorifies the physical and promises recognition as reward for overcoming fear. These people get recognition from others, but less of that feeling of self-worth that comes after putting months into something where you are dependent only upon yourself, and prey to hopes and doubts.

Solo Climb of Nanga Parbat

Only in 1978 after I learned that life can be endured alone did I have the courage to make the solo climb of Nanga Parbat, the greatest leap forward in my climbing career. Alone I climbed a new route on the Diamir Face without technical aids. When an earthquake triggered avalanches, the narrow tongue of ice I had followed the previous day to scale the middle section of the face was erased completely. It had peeled off and plunged to the bottom of the mountain. Clearly, I could not go back the same way. Despite the fact that my retreat had been cut off, I was in good spirits. I was aware that only luck had saved me, but I pressed on as if luck itself bred more luck. I felt as though I were a spirit, immune from physical harm. I no longer had any fear at all. There was no going back, only forward. In a state of exaltation, I climbed on. The sky above seemed like black eternity. With every upward step it opened ever wider, interrupted only by that wedge, white against the dark background, of the summit soaring above me. On August 9, I finally reached the summit, and I returned from summit to base camp by a different new route.

Lonely at the Top

In summer 1979, after K2, I experienced a fresh wave of antipathy. I felt more lonely on this pinnacle of celebrity than ever before. Even friends withdrew further from me. The press reacted critically. Although K2 had never been climbed by so small a team before, nor as quickly, this expedition was interpreted as a "deviation" from my usual style, even though we climbed without oxygen masks and placed no camps or fixed rope on the upper sections, and even though we operated without Sherpas. I have never sought to be a folk hero and was accustomed to rejection. All the same, it was not always easy to cope with so much misunderstanding. I felt no great temptation to ingratiate myself with the critics; I thought it better to keep quiet. Recognition was less important than remaining true to myself, especially when swimming alone against the tide.

Restless Anticipation

Restlessly I anticipate the coming days in a half-awake condition. Partly with curiosity, partly in fear, I await the dawn. I know the dangers that await me up there: crevasses, avalanches, mists, and storms. I know above all my own weaknesses: exhaustion, fear, and loneliness.

Need for Security

In the long stops for breathing, something like homesickness comes over me. My need for security overcomes me, and with that I know that all hopes that someone waits for me down below are, like the anxiety before my solo climb, impeding and even paralyzing. Only when moving, only when seeking and seeing, does it become possible for me to accept this loneliness. When I think, the energy at my disposal is quickly used up. With will-power alone, I can progress no further now; but when I disengage my brain, I am open to a power outside myself. I am like a hollow hand and experience a regeneration. The "clenched fist" contributes to my exhaustion and loneliness. Only when I am like a hollow hand with out-stretched fingers does an invisible part of my being regenerate, not only in sleep, but also in climbing.

Born to Be Alone?

With inactivity, my self-understanding and my self-confidence shrink. Perhaps that is the reason why I so wonder about the hermits—because through meditation they can survive loneliness. It is hardest to endure the wilderness in idleness. So, is man born to go alone? To go alone at times,

Pg. 1: Karakorum, Broad Peak, summit. Hours on the summit are rarely this peaceful. Once on top, you can only climb down and then up again.

Pg. 2: Karakorum, K2, summit walk. Every step toward the summit are two steps away from civilization.

Pg. 3: Karakorum, Gasherbrum II, summit. A short breather between ascent and descent.

Above: Himalaya, Annapurna I. To get through the chaos of the ice break, creativity is needed.

Below: Himalaya, Annapurna I. A roped party consists of people who are all equally enthusiatic for the adventure

Right: When cold, stress and fear last for days, endurance counts.

Below: Karakorum, Abruzzi-Glacier. Porters marching to the base camp.

Above: Himalaya, Broad Peak. An 8,000-meter mountain requires logical thinking, determination, and a willingness to take chances.

Below: Karakorum, Gasherbrum I, on the summit ridge in a storm. Life on knife's edge.

Right: Karakorum, Gasherbrum II. A path has to be cleared.

Previous double page: Himalaya, Annapurna I. Lost in the crevice of the ice. But there is always a way either up or down.

Above: Karakorum, K2. Halfway to the summit.

Below left: Himalaya, Dhaulagiri. At the summit: storm, cold, but no panic.

Above: Karakorum. On the way to Concordia. Often the success of an expedition is determined on the approach.

Below: Himalaya, Annapurna I; Northwest Wall. Lost in a vertical wilderness. Hanging on a large wall is an adventure

Far left: Karakorum, K2, House-chimney. Difficulties exist so that they can be overcome.

Left: Himalaya, Annapurna I; passage into the Northwest Wall. Every meter counts.

Below: Himalaya, Annapurna I; ice wall under the shoulder at the end of the Northwest Wall. Tolerance for mistakes: zero!

Above: Karakorum, ascent on Gasherbrum II. Only motivation, stored up in advance, lasts for days in the death zone.

Below: Karakorum, Gasherbrum II. This leads nowhere, but we can turn back.

Next page: Karakorum, approach. To lead a column of porters is like managing a small enterprise

Last page: Himalaya, Annapurna. The first successful ascent in 1950 was led by a mad man.

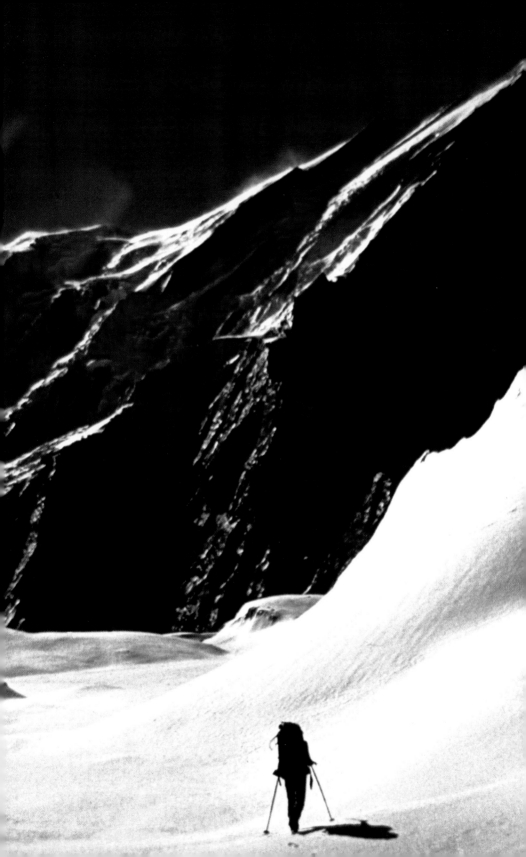

yes, but not to be alone. And yet how quickly I shut myself off from others! How inept in sharing expectations and accomplishments, much preferring to climb alone, and at times preferring to be alone.

Fear of Being Alone

Although I am in the best shape of my life in my attempt to climb Broad Peak alone, I can't cope with being alone. I cannot get through the walk to it. I call off the "smallest possible 8,000-meter climb." I also give up my second attempt at a solo ascent of Nanga Parbat—turn back already during the approach! I am too weak mentally. I must first be capable of autonomy in all other areas of life. I know that in 1973, 1974, and 1977 I failed because of fear of being alone in the border region. Still, going alone is often easier than a group trip, since the main imponderables depend on me alone. Once I have made a decision as a solo hiker, I can either stick to it firmly or change it rapidly, as circumstances so require. It depends on me alone. Still, I am skeptical about "solo adventures" that are almost never done in groups. Going alone must remain the exception.

A solo traveler cannot share his joys and fears. In a limit situation, the lack cannot be seen in any other human face. Schizophrenia is often the last salvation. The ability let yourself be divided into parts, between A and B, harmony and dialectic, must be learned. The lack of partners in solo situations must be replaced by the ability to split yourself into two or more personalities.

Solo climbs are not especially difficult to plan; but the ability to hike alone requires much more than perfection in planning and execution. In addition to the corresponding idea and motivation, I need first of all the ability to live, and to be alone. Loneliness is one of the central problems of people. It can be especially acute in border-crossers, between the high feeling of independence and the specter of abandonment.

Being alone and loneliness are not the same thing. Being alone triggers opposite feelings—according to whether it is being experienced voluntarily or by force. Loneliness is also always accompanied by a feeling of abandonment, being lost. This feeling of being lost and abandoned leads rapidly to the darkness of meaninglessness, in which time stands still.

Preparation for Solo Climb

This time I have myself under control. I give fear no chance from the outset. The most dangerous part of the route, the ascent to the North Col, I know already, and as far as that is concerned I could only get stuck in the snow or lose myself in the mist, but not perish. The weather is fine, there will be no mist! My self-control costs energy. I sense how keyed-up my body is. Even during the night, I have to force myself to lie quietly. Only twice do I look out at the weather. It is fine, but the air is too warm. In the blue of the night, Mount Everest stands over me like a magic mountain. No pondering, no asking why, I prepare myself with every fibre of my being for the big effort.

When it is time to get up I pick up socks, boots, breeches, and top clothes like a sleep-walker. Each movement is quick and sure, as if I had practiced them a hundred times. No wasted movement. This time there is no one to help carry; no one to prepare my bivouac; no comrade to help me break trail in deep snow; and no Sherpa to carry my equipment. Nobody. How much easier it is to climb as a pair. The knowledge that someone is standing behind you brings comfort. Not only is solo climbing far more strenuous and dangerous, the psychological burden is more than doubled.

All Out of Proportion

While resting, everything that lies ahead of me, including the descent, is all blown up, all out of proportion, weighing me down. Like a snail which carries its home on its back, I carry my tent in my rucksack. I shall erect it, sleep in it, and take it with me for the next night. I am equipped like a nomad. I can survive for a week. Nevertheless I have scarcely any reserves. After seven days I must be back—nothing can be allowed to go wrong. A second tent would be too heavy, to say nothing of oxygen apparatus, which would double my load again. My 18 kilos weighs so heavily at this height that I now stop and stand after every two dozen steps, struggle for breath, and forget everything around me.

The stretches between the rest stops become shorter and shorter. Often I sit down to have a breather. Each time it takes greater will-power to stand up again. The knowledge that I have completed my self-inflicted day's stint helps me now. It is as if thinking of that releases energy. "Still a bit more, you can do it," I say to myself softly by way of encouragement. "What you climb today, you won't have to climb tomorrow."

Soloing doesn't feel like isolation now. Only occasionally does a feeling of impotence strike me with the thought of the awful endless exertion which still lies before me. If a friend, a partner, were there we could alternate with breaking trail. Physically I am carrying the exertion alone. Psychologically I imagine helpers, someone behind me! Is it my separated ego or some other human energy which compensates for a partner? Thus, with this phantom, am I accompanied up to a height of 8,000 meters. **MM**

* * *

Application and Action:

Application: In an era of teams and co-leaders, the art of being alone and climbing alone may sound passé, if not anachronistic. But Messner makes a strong case for doing all you can by and for yourself, not out of selfish motives but rather selfless motives—engaging in risky activity in service of the shared objective. His ideas serve as a reminder that teams don't work unless every individual member assumes personal responsibility for desired results.

Action: Determine what can best be done by acting alone, pioneering new ground in a solo effort, and what can best be done by working in a group. Plan a "solo" venture of your own and record what you learn from the experience. **AA**

Chapter 15
Failure, Tragedy, and Death

In any high adventure, you are likely to meet failure, tragedy, and even death. And when your career spans decades and dozens of risky climbs, you see and meet it all. In this chapter, Messner bares his soul. He talks of failure and tells of surviving multiple tragedies. Having spent several days, not just minutes, in the "death zone," he writes with authority on the subject. He knows first hand how fragile life can be, how quickly it can be extinguished, and how hard it is to fight back from failure and from the death of brothers and close companions. Between the lines, Messner is telling us all how to prepare for and meet our own inevitable death— and even how to rise again from near-death experiences.

* * *

Failure: Hitting the Wall

When we come to a wall in life, the impending failure mobilizes forces in us, forces that we do not know beforehand. When we fail, this wall often gets larger. It repeatedly energizes us to find new combinations to solve problems. Suddenly something previously considered impossible is possible. Never fear failure by retreat. The fear of failure is there before the start of my expeditions, but never with the retreat from them, nor immediately after the failure. When rappelling from a wall without achieving the summit, it is naturally clear to me that I have "lost."

Death of Brother, Gunther

On 27 July 1970, first climbing separately and then together, my brother Gunther and I reached the summit of Nanga Parbat. We had climbed the Rupal Face, the highest rock and ice wall in the world. During the final stages of this supreme effort, both of us were at the limits of our endurance. In our youthful enthusiasm, we were prepared to push things further than ever I would now. It was late in the day when we reached the summit. My brother was extremely tired and exhibiting the first signs of altitude sickness. I could see that he wasn't able to go much further. In that condition it would have been irresponsible, if not impossible, to try and shepherd him back down the Rupal Face. Especially as we did not have a rope with us. There was no way of safeguarding Gunther. He would almost certainly have fallen somewhere on the way down.

Late that afternoon, in gathering cloud, I decided we should retreat down the West Face as far as the notch above the Merkl Gully. It was a short-term measure; I believed we could get back to the Rupal Face from there the next morning, and hoped that by then there would be other climbers who could assist us. Thus, we waited out the long and dreadful night. We were at a height of 8,000-meters and had no bivouac equipment: no down jackets, no oxygen, nothing to eat or drink. It was a night that undermined us totally, physically and psychologically.

The next morning I could see we were not fit to go anywhere, certainly not all the way down the mountain. And when, after waiting till about 10 o'clock, we were forced to accept that Peter Scholz and Felix Kuen were not on their way to help us but were going for the summit themselves, we began, in desperation, to descend the Diamir side of Nanga Parbat.

I was nearly out of my mind, and it was at this point that I fell down and felt my spirit leave my body. In a perfectly detached fashion I watched myself roll down the mountain. But then, summoning up one last surge of effort, I forced myself back into my body—I had to get my brother down to safety.

The Diamir side is not as steep as the Rupal Face. From above, it looked feasible and offered the only solution to our predicament, albeit a slim and transitory one. I could not bear the idea of dying in inactivity. We would at least make a last, desperate attempt to get down. We struggled on until after midnight. I kept having to wait for Gunther, to guide him through seracs and down the rocks of the Mummery Rib.

By the third day of this nerve-racking descent we were well down, where the glacier levels off. I was out in front, scouting the route, and Gunther failed to catch up. When I went back, I saw that a huge avalanche had come down since I'd passed that way. I knew immediately that Gunther must be buried beneath it, that I was alone. But I could not accept that he was dead. He had been with me on hundreds of difficult routes. It was unthinkable that we would never be together again! With him, I had always had the feeling that we were bound together. How could he leave me here alone among these high valleys, these rocks and icefalls?

A whole day and night I looked for him. In the frozen rubble of this glacier world, parched, with frost-bitten hands and feet, I made my first acquaintance with madness. I no longer knew nor cared where I was, nor what I did. I could barely walk. Even so, I stumbled on, painfully slowly. It was only when I met some wood-cutters who showed me the way to the valley, that I woke from the limbo where death had been walking a few steps ahead of me.

It took many years to get over the death of my brother, to accommodate his death as part of my life. I had first to learn to live with the tragedy. In the autumn of 1970 I had six toes and the tips of several fingers amputated in the University Clinic in Innsbruck. At that time, I never believed I would go back to the mountains. Nor did I want to. The distress of my parents and brothers and sister made me realize just how much of a burden climbers inflict upon those who love them. My mother begged me never to go to an 8,000-meter peak again.

Tragedy and Agony

Manaslu was my second 8,000-meter mountain (1972), and a second tragedy. For the second time, I lost the will to go back—but only briefly. I was devastated by the loss of my friends and the renewed frost-bite, and did not believe I could bear the agony of going up an 8,000er a third time—and coming back alive.

No Reversing Death

Until 1972, I had lived just to climb mountains—with considerable ambition, with the resolve to employ as little in the way of technical aid as possible, with the notion of pushing beyond all the accepted limits of the time. I had been going my own way. From a study of Alpine history, I had extracted my own philosophies. The loss of my brother—and other friends—shocked me into real consciousness of just how closely mountaineering is linked with death, how dangerous it is. I hadn't really thought about it before. A climber who does not understand that death is a possible outcome of any serious climb is a fool. I learned, too, that there was nothing I could do to reverse the tragedies on Nanga Parbat and Manaslu.

Inevitability of Death

Death, the inevitability of death, has played no leading part in my sensations. And yet perhaps it is that too which determines my behavior. Never have I come so near my limit, the limit between this side and that side, between self and other, as on my solo ascent of Everest. Never has a mountain expedition influenced me so enduringly as this one. Perhaps I have crossed the Rubicon and made a leap which I have still to absorb. The week-long struggle for survival in that hostile environment has altered me. The overwhelming landscape has made me still more of an individualist, detached from humanity, perhaps even morbidly absorbed in fantasy.

Failure, Tragedy, and Death

The Point of No Return

I am not entirely free myself from the fear of death, although I have experienced near-death, even the feeling of having died once. In these intense near-death situations, I have learned much about life. In a sense, after every intense situation, a new life starts for me. I experience a kind of rebirth. For physical reasons, my time is limited. At 60 years of age, I can no longer climb Mount Everest without oxygen equipment or reach the North Pole "unsupported." My speed, energy, and health are declining. Ice-crossing, an endurance sport, involves not so much physical performance ability as mental calmness. And this grows with age. In border situations—cold, hunger, tiredness—many young people die first, even though they are stronger than the older ones. For example, seven people died within a few days on K2 in 1986, but the three oldest survived. It is still important for me to experience whether I can still go beyond myself: how ambition, instincts, and fear function at the "point of no return."

Life Is Intense in the Death Zone

Our undertaking could easily have turned out very differently. We don't think about that. In the Death Zone, success and disaster run as closely together as storm and lull, hot and cold. Of the seven times I have attempted an 8,000-meter peak, I have only four times reached the summit. Now I appreciate that. As in all true adventure, the path between the summit and the grave is a very narrow one indeed. That there is no way of telling in advance which way it will finish, does not mean that life up there is any more significant, but it is certainly more intense.

Can't Linger in the Death Zone

At extreme altitudes, we can only have success if with go without any intermediate stops. A long stay in the "death zone" always means a loss of concentration, will, strength, and energy. Even if we are prepared to endure any discomfort, and forego any protection against the unknown, that does not include placing life itself at risk—since we know that we may be lost in so doing.

We get along better than we thought. It was the fear of defeat that paralyzed us, and not a suspicion that it might cost us our lives. In early morning, we are at the top. For a while, I am completely alone. I am as if in a trance. It is as if I had stepped out of time to think in a complex and new way, even if only very slowly. Nevertheless, I experience no mood of success. With the realization of my plan, I also have to give up my utopia. I miss it as a supporting feeling. An emptiness remains.

Close to Death

The closest I ever came to death on a mountain still remains my experience on the Nanga Parbat crossing of 1970, my first ascent of an 8,000er. Taking into account difficulties, effort, danger, and hopelessness, no other adventure has superseded that one. I even believe that it would no longer be possible for anyone to traverse Nanga Parbat in the way Gunther and I did in 1970. Perhaps if 1,000 climbers tried, one might come through. I am sure that I could never survive those days a second time.

The Limit of Endurance

My climb with Friedl Mutschlechner of Kangchenjunga's North Face was one of the most dangerous of my life. It was the timing of the storm more than anything else that brought us close to the limit of our endurance. We were already suffering sickness and frost-bite. The storm hammered us just as we tired, coming down from the summit, when we had lost the curiosity that is the driving force on the way up. And it broke so violently it practically swept us from the mountain. It almost succeeded in extinguishing our spirit of life.

The fool is not the person who goes up there in full knowledge that this kind of climbing is hazardous, but the one who does not want to know about death, who shuts his eyes to the fact that he could be killed. Who among us is crazy? No one risks his life for a sponsor. But many people consciously accept risk to experience wilderness like this. Adventure without risk is impossible.

Success Beyond Failure

Having proved my tactics could work without disaster, I was convinced that I could climb more 8,000ers in the same manner. I was not going to be stopped by the criticism, nor even by the failure of my marriage, which it precipitated. At no other time did a challenge appear as logical to me, as when I juxtaposed the existence of an 8,000er with my fantasies. It was ludicrous to suggest I climbed only for profit. I was a dreamer and have stayed a dreamer. I have never ceased to put new ideas into practice and will give up my activities only when they hold nothing more for me, not just when there is nothing more to be earned from them.   **MM**

✳   ✳   ✳

Application and Action:

Application: Since we all experience failure and tragedy in life and business, we can learn much from Messner in this chapter. By learning how to cope with failure and recover from setbacks, we create comebacks. In your organization, you might identify areas where comebacks are needed and decide how to escape imminent disaster.

Action: Look at your life and work and determine how you can best apply the lessons you have learned from down times to produce better times.   **AA**

Survival in Storm

by Friedl Mutschlecher, climber of three 8,000ers

On the way down the mountain, the storm assumes hurricane proportions, taking all our concentration to find the way and reach the security of the tent without mishap. Despite the euphoria, I feel tired and worn out. Each of us has given the climb his all, and for this reason the storm now seems to hit us harder.

All hell is let loose. Driving snow lashes into our faces. We can't see a thing. Even so, we manage to get back to our tent before the onset of darkness. We leave our crampons outside and crawl into our icy sleeping bags with our boots on. The storm rages on with such ferocity it is impossible to cook anything, or to sleep—as sleep would surely be the end. Sitting with our backs to the walls of the tent, we endeavor to withstand the force of the wind. We have pitifully little with which to counter its effects.

At some stage I notice my right hand has lost all feeling—the fingers are frozen stiff. I must not give up, on any account. I concentrate everything on this one thought. All sense of time is lost. Minutes become hours; hours, eternity.

We dare not make the slightest error. Vainly I shout for help, but even Reinhold, who is sitting beside me, cannot hear me over the noise of the storm. The tent-front rips on a pole. We look at each other, knowing what can happen. With my hands, I make a sign to Reinhold to brace himself more firmly against the side. A shiver of fright passes through me. I fear the worst.

I speak all my thoughts aloud. That way I can maintain better control over myself. My concentration diminishes markedly. I wonder to what extent I am still thinking clearly. The thought of dying no longer frightens me. Death has become a tangible option; it would not be that bad, lying down and dying. The temptation to take that tiny step towards eternal sleep is enormous. Then the tent rips, and suddenly we are lying in the open air. "Lucky we left our boots on," I think, but my thoughts come in slow motion. A last convulsion of strength allows me to put on my crampons. The wind keeps toppling me over as I do it. I notice Ang Dorje, our trusted Sherpa, is having the same trouble. We begin the climb down together—without Reinhold.

Below the ridge I look for somewhere to shelter and wait for Reinhold. Obviously he must be having trouble. I shout myself hoarse that he come quickly, but the storm is too loud for him to hear. He keeps falling over. I would like to help him, but haven't the strength to climb back up, even that short distance. The only thing I can do is not leave him on his own. Each of us knows that in situations like this, you are your own responsibility—there is only strength for yourself.

All I can do is wait, helplessly, watching him struggle. It is a question of survival. It would come very hard if to save yourself, you were forced to leave a partner behind in such situations, but that is the reality. Each has the right, perhaps even the duty, to do just that. Reinhold's attitude of mind has helped him to survive many other adventures, and I believe it will see him through this one. No one knows better than he that no one here can help him.

I have no idea how long it takes before he is standing next to me. Without a word, we continue down. Only when the Sherpas in Camp 2 greet us with hot tea do we know that we have survived.

The Double Traverse

by Hans Kammerlander, climber of seven 8,000ers

In my opinion, traversing the two Gasherbrum summits ranks as one of the hardest tours ever done. At the same time, stylistically, it was one of the purest climbs made on an 8,000er.

The most important factor was the length of time we spent at very high altitude. We were treading new ground, unknown territory—not just in the mountaineering and geographical sense but also in an emotional sense. Other factors too, played their part. For instance, our medical, psychological, and technological reactions to such a ride. Eight days in the "Death Zone" without going back to Base Camp amount to more than that when you consider the critical circumstances: a week of hard physical effort with insufficient sleep, no fixed ropes, and little knowledge of the territory to be covered. I believe that every new frontier situation, whether on a mountain, in art or science or business, signifies a small revolution for existing standards and semantics.

Reinhold once wrote 10 commandments for responsible mountaineering: boots with profile soles, spare underwear, personal identification, two prussik slings, toilet paper. . . . The Alpine catechism, you might say. The book outlines the approach that Reinhold teaches in his climbing school. He has taken it to absurd lengths himself. We set off for the Gasherbrums with no climbing or sit harnesses, no compass, and no helmets. Candles and medical kit found a place in our equipments, but the 20 meters of 6mm line hardly constituted rope.

A heretical father-superior with his apprentice? Two climbing outlaws who cannot obey the most elementary regulation? Certainly not! The Gasherbrum-Traverse Project was not realized by employing the found rules of classical mountaineering. Only

143

the rucksack—packed according to the commandment of theoretical safety—could not be dispensed with.

For this traverse, which took eight days of our lives, we played by the rules of the Messneric Koran (we were after all in Pakistan). We left all the book doctrine behind us to attempt what popular opinion deemed impossible. Our success proved us right, and if I now recall certain instances of the traverse, it is to point up where the text books need extending—not rewriting, just expanding.

It was our fourth climbing day when we began the descent of Gasherbrum II, down a steep, crevassed hanging glacier. Common sense would most certainly have declared this forbidden territory. Yet we came safely down because we climbed in the very early morning on hard-frozen ice. The previous day we had given up the whole afternoon because we needed to come down this section at the most favorable time—first thing in the morning. We climbed unroped. There are not many other climbers who can crampon down as quickly and nimbly as Reinhold Messner.

Two days later, coming off the summit snowfield of Gasherbrum I, Reinhold took a bad fall. He peeled off backwards into space and was away. I have known people, trained sports climbers, who in such a situation would not have come to rest till they hit the deck. But Reinhold was able to fling himself round in mid-air so that he was facing downwards, and then regain his footing several meters lower on steep, glazed rock slabs. It's not for me to eulogize here over this 40-year-old, beset at the time with all sorts of aches and pains; suffice it to say that quick reactions and balance like that aren't sold in any sports shop.

Further down, just before the glacier leveled out, we were nearly wiped out by a rock avalanche which came straight for us out of the mist. A huge rock pillar had collapsed on the ridge above. Why were we not killed? Sheer luck!

People always take issue with us over the "signal" power of tours like this—according to your viewpoint, they can be seen as setting good or bad examples. It is alleged that it encourages young people into this kind of adventure, to take such risks. Reinhold has always rejected such arguments, believing in freedom of choice and the common sense of the individual.

Peak performances in any branch of life are not available by prescription, nor are they transferable one to another. The product of talent, intelligence, instinct and hard work is usually only sufficient for one activity, for one single exercise.

Section IV

✳ ✳ ✳

Overcoming Challenges

Having documented in Section III the many challenges that we face in any attempt at the summit, we now turn with Messner to the best ways to overcome these challenges. He expands on the idea of risk management. Included in this curriculum is a crash course in the high ideology of "fair means" and the low technology of preparation and training. He provides us with clear insight and with a creative approach to climbing any mountain. Here the parallels between life and mountaineering are most evident, as Messner outlines the mindset, the methodology, and the personal qualities that accompany innovation, creative expression, path-breaking, and pioneering. Within these chapters we can find the solutions we need to climb our mountains.

Chapter 16
Fair Means

In this chapter, Messner elucidates the ethic of "fair means"—his way of climbing and living. He approaches the mountain as a man without bottled oxygen and high technology and leaves the mountain clean, without the litter of a major encampment. In this way, Messner satisfies his own sense of mission and gains an increased measure of self-respect. We can all benefit from the lessons taught here, whatever our occupations. The tenet that why and how we do our business matter as much as what we do is under attack today—an age of moral relativism and legal maneuvering. Messner keeps moral, ethical, and social responsibility for his actions squarely with himself. His insistence on doing the right things at the right time in the right way has greatly enlarged his legacy.

*　　*　　*

Summit Trophies

We may poke fun at ourselves as "conquistadors of the useless," but we continue to stuff our rucksacks with the baggage of heroics, summit-fever, and the lust for conquest. Even with Sherpas and guides preparing the route and bearing all responsibility for a climb, today's high-altitude tourists increasingly return to the valley sporting their "success" as an award for valor. I have learned that a summit never belongs to you—certainly not once you come down from it. Never. And yet, seemingly, you can "buy" it, lay claim to it, even when not up there. This basic truth in a preeminently capitalistic world is not one that high-altitude climbers care to concede. New ideals keep being devised to justify invasion of their blue mountains. Thus even the huge gulf between the mythical concept of "the Mountain" and mass tourism on the roof of the world can be assimilated into the mind-set of people who have lost the ability to criticize themselves.

Climbing as a Man

All my 8,000ers were climbed without oxygen masks—in the same way as I have never in my life used an expansion bolt. I imposed that rule on myself in the Alps when I first began extreme climbing. Expansion bolts make it theoretically possible to eliminate uncertainly, the very element that gives climbing its excitement. It is precisely this "perhaps it's not possible" question that is so important. I would have felt cheated if, from the outset, I had canceled out that uncertainty with some technical device. In 1978 I knew I could climb to 8,500 meters using oxygen, but I did not want to do it. Instead, I wanted to know how far I might push into this "perhaps it's not possible" territory as a man, not as a man-machine, using my own strengths and resources, notwithstanding any doubts or debilitations I might have.

Fair Means Philosophy

I refuse to ruin this challenge through the use of technological aids. To survive in this epoch of depersonalization, concrete deserts, and the alienation brought about by being harnessed into the crazy machinery of manufacturing, management and administration, I need the mountains as an alternative world. If you fail to understand my despair and think that my "fair means" philosophy is an over-subtle indulgence, I invite you to take a trip to the Everest base camp of today by the Khumbu ice-fall. When you see the vast rubbish heap left there by previous mountaineers from the West with their throwaway technology, then you will understand me.

Nothing to Fall Back On

I comprehend what it means to be without the help of oxygen equipment, to be climbing heavenwards without a breathing mask to fall back on. Perhaps that is what is worrying me, and perhaps too because by the light of the moon, all the difficulties, the dimensions and the exertions involved, always seem to be doubled. I keep imagining the slopes above, recalling the harsh nights I spent stormbound on the South Col. It would be an easy thing to climb Everest with oxygen. This I know because many men and women who are far from peak condition still manage to do it in good time and fine style. I climbed Everest in Alpine style when it was thought to be completely impossible without oxygen and no one dared guess in what state someone would come back from the summit.

Amateurs and Imposters

I ask other climbers to dispense with substantial technical aids. By that I mean oxygen gear, expansion bolts, helicopters—in short, gear with which the impossible may be made not only possible but rather common. I would rather cope with the mountain by using my own abilities and not by relying on technology. "By fair means" has been replaced by "any means whatsoever" as the motto of those advertising strategists who make a living out of demeaning Mount Everest. Is it any wonder that the summit has been increasingly "open for business" and the rubbish dumps at base camp have been piling higher? Beware those travel operators who only want to fill their group tours!

The blame cannot be laid at Sir Edmund Hillary's door for triggering this boom on "his" mountain; it comes down to us, my generation, and the many empty-headed mountain-addicts, who seek to equate altitude with quality, babbling on about "summit-luck in the death-zone." As the market for it came into being, a generation of Sunday climbers with no experience of hunger or cold, wore a footpath to the roof of the world: men and women, amateurs and imposters.

Possibilities of Pioneering

Today's Everest is no longer the Everest of pioneers. Increasingly the apex of vanity, Everest has also become a substitute for something the summit-traveler wants to flaunt on his lapel, like a badge, without taking any of the responsibility in the field. The more Everest is turned into a consumer article, the more importance attaches to the key moments of its climbing history—with or without supplemental oxygen. As the highest mountain in the world—for trekkers, climbers, environmentalists, and aid workers (to say nothing of undertakers)—it is guaranteed more publicity than any other mountain. Its mythos is continually being misinterpreted, so that it becomes a mountain of fortune and fantasy even for those with no need to go there themselves. For them, I tell my story of climbing by fair means. There are still possibilities of a pioneering nature waiting to be done on Mount Everest—even today—should anyone be looking for them. But who cares to take on the challenge of exposure and loneliness away from the beaten track when the summit can be "bagged" so much more easily?

Social Responsibility

All climbers have a great responsibility toward the subsequent generations. None of us has the right to tie up the 8,000ers with fixed ropes, to put in high camps, and then leave them untidily behind. Of course, we all have a right to climb, each where we will and on any conceivable route. But at the same time, we have the duty to take back down the mountain everything we have carried up. We must learn to leave mountains as we find them. That is the only way they can remain thrilling and interesting places for the people following after, and continue to afford the fascinating challenge that we needed—and the challenge that future young mountaineers will need every bit as much. Our generation is not going to be measured by how many 8,000ers we bagged and how fast we made the climbs; we will be remembered for how intact we leave these mountains as places of opportunity for the next generation. A South Pillar clean of pegs and ropes will still hold interest in later years; a South Pillar heavy with protection is not merely boring, it is repellent. **MM**

* * *

Application and Action:

Application: We would all like a good shortcut to the top, complete with social acclaim. And so the "trophy" climb and the "Everest industry" are booming. But Messner argues passionately for a more personal, responsible, and artistic approach to climbing. In making application of his ethical principle, you might examine the why and how of your work.

Action: Invent and implement a way to do your work with less waste, fanfare, and artificial aid. Seek an authentic and ethical way to achieve your goals. **AA**

Chapter 17

Preparation and Training, Learning, Growing, Changing

The Scout motto of "Be Prepared" only partly applies in the Messner "bias for action" book. He may rewrite the motto: Be as prepared as you possibly can—and then expect the unexpected, be flexible, and adapt on the spot to situational realities. Of course, he believes in planning and preparation, teaching and training, but not so much in the formal classroom as on the face of the mountain. There is nothing quite like on-the-job experience and on-site adventure to stimulate real learning, growth, and change. Messner's concept of planning is minimal calculation and anticipated decision-making. He advises us to train and plan and prepare but also to leave ourselves open to influence and inner voices once on the mountain.

✳ ✳ ✳

Preparation

I have never fooled myself about my expeditions to the highest summits of this earth. I have always known that something could go wrong, but at the same time I have prepared myself for the conceivable dangers and planned in detail what to do in such circumstances.

Training

Only if a climber keeps forcing himself to train, if he lets himself be driven by his own fanaticism to the outposts of his potential, can these limits be moved—his personal limits, that is, as well as the limits of Alpine climbing. To be fully stretched means being in perpetual momentum, being dragged along. Only thus is the climber capable of dismantling the inner barriers when he finds himself, after months of work and preparation, at the foot of a big wall. Only thus can he cope with the isolation, the apprehension, and the spells of faintness that are much harder to overcome than all the rocks in the world. Good fortune and benign providence are presents from the gods, as the Tibetans say; they are an extra. But the prerequisites for success the climber has to acquire for himself—they are never given freely, anywhere.

Change and Grow

Change in order to progress. Avoid the burnout syndrome. Phase transitions. Start new activities at the right moment. Life requires a paradigm switch: Optimal output through change to a new life phase. Always begin anew with young people. Start playing as a way to rejuvenate yourself. Man has no permanent occupation. Man has no duties other than those wished on himself. Influences come from both the outside and from inside yourself. Latent discontent can be unbuilt with the courage to go where it drives you. Be yourself. Our crisis is a crisis of being satisfied with the status quo.

Change and Progress

Change is a rejuvenating cure. If I want to progress, I must face many new beginnings. I do not see this progression as a "higher" duty. It is a self-provided demand—a demand on myself. A person has no "higher" duty on this earth, except for the responsibility for one's family, for friends (which are wanted themselves), and the common responsibility of the community. We do have the right, however, to want these things for ourselves, to give ourselves such challenges.

Planning Elements

Minimum calculation is a possibility. Planning is anticipated decision-making. In theory, I can plan everything. Computers can simulate everything. I plan without strict guidelines, using negative abstraction processes. I employ only a few planning elements. Knowing when the plan can't work can save your life. Cornerstones of planning include quality, costs, and time. Flexibility stands between planning and execution. I champion on-site improvisation, the elimination of bottlenecks, minimal help and technology, and cleaner, fairer, more human adventures. I leave my plan for life open.

Growth Potential

Everyone can grow beyond himself. Competitive situations require instinct and ambition. Total energy is more than the sum of individual energies. I use self-reliance and helplessness as motivation aids when I reach the "point of no return." Only when I can get along with myself can I try to get along with others. I don't climb to get to the top. I get to the top after I have climbed. Anyone who has become who he is can do anything he wants; also because he only wants what he can do.

Training for the Tour

Whenever I felt I was lacking in strength or stamina, I intensified my training. My will, too, was schooled by this same long training, and by the climbing itself. Failure gave me the incentive to go on, to better earlier achievements with each new step; but in this, I could only hope to succeed if my powers of concentration, my commitment, and my knowledge kept expanding. My climbing activities no longer aroused the same interest as they did in 1978—they had become too frequent, perhaps too successful. That worried me less than the knowledge that I could not live for any length of time without the stimulus of extreme experience. My motivations were no longer the same as they had been on Nanga Parbat in 1970; without doubt they were stronger. There was no question of giving up.

To climb 8,000ers is less a matter of skill and know-how, which is what rock climbing demands; far more, it requires an optimum combination of endurance, will-power, and instinct, and an ability to tolerate suffering. The right thing to do at any given moment is only learned over decades. You can compare an expedition like this with the Tour de France or Giro d'Italia. These long competitions last for weeks and exact the utmost from cyclists every day of that time.   MM

*   *   *

Application and Action:

Application: When faced with a tough challenge, we need to intensify our training and conditioning. In our planning and preparation, we need to anticipate conceivable dangers. We can then adapt the plan as needed once we encounter actual conditions.

Action: Engage in the degree of training, planning, and preparation demanded by the difficulty of your task.   AA

Chapter 18

Innovation and Creative Expression

Innovation and creative expression are keys to success in any real-world endeavor. In this substantive chapter, Messner extols the merits of revolutionary ideas, innovative actions, and creative expressions—all part of the chain of steps to overcoming challenges. If you take old ideas and a fixed approach into the field, expect to fall behind the innovator who is converting new thinking into fresh approaches and meaningful actions. Messner calls creativity the "divine characteristic" because for him it has often spelled the difference between life and death on the mountain. His bag of "creativity tricks" include everything from taking a cold shower to relaxing, dreaming, visualizing and disengaging to allow new ideas to enter the mind.

✳   ✳   ✳

Revolutionary Ideas

Out of nebulous intentions and idealistic willpower comes a sense of urgency, and then a concrete action reality. With this, a doubly bold experiment is possible: Disturbing the comfortable old order in expeditions and introducing a new system. I do not want to be simply an administrator on my expedition, but an architect and pioneer. Developing new strategies is more important for me than reaching the top.

We need to be strong through simplicity in strategy and fast in operating equipment. No longer will budgets, size of the group, and materials be used determine success, but the

157

quality of the group, the know-how, and the power of innovation. Today we have the means and the freedom to go everywhere we want. But we do not have the right to sell our culture, our knowledge, and our religion anywhere as the best or to force them onto other people. We should not hurry too much, but we should also not sleep through our opportunities to reach the top. Our strategy is to stay alert. We have trust in each other, self-assurance, and sufficient acclimatization. And so we seek the summit. We reduce equipment and provisions to a bare minimum, hoping to be back in three or four days. To accomplish a new idea, we must above all have the courage to think in a revolutionary way: first the idea, then the method of implementation, lastly risk management. In action, I know what is right and what is wrong.

My Game Rules

I moved away from the old expedition form: Self-responsibility instead of the pyramid system (two to the summit). Maturation process: This is my goal, my style, my essence. Simple structure: Idea and logistics fit on one piece of paper. How do I get from A to B? A pioneering performance in the adventure cannot be planned with a computer. I don't expect perfection in my relationships; rather, I strive for solutions to problems in teams, materials, and minimizing weight and time duration. I start a trend toward smaller undertakings. Redundancy makes adventure difficult. Have no fear of fear. Decide and act according to facts.

Self-Made Rules

All kinds of rules are suspicious to me—excepts self-made rules. The fact that I drew up my own game rules for my adventures does not say that these game rules must apply to everyone else. Without rules, however, there is no game. Now, as I toss out ballast and shorten the train, I can walk and climb elegantly and live how I want to live: a feeling of being on my own, and living by my own rules. To follow one's own rhythm is more valuable than joint success. Anyone who has functioned as a "little wheel" in a large expedition, obliged to follow the orders of an expedition leader and devote himself to the expedition, knows that possibilities for play and experience are greater in small, light expeditions.

Innovative Strategy

Thinking dogmatically and behaving in the usual way should be prevented. Why couldn't my new expedition style become faster, promise more success, and be less dangerous? There are few men in the game. We few men could react faster to outbreaks of bad weather and get down the mountain faster, then climb up again faster than is possible with a large group.

The strategy of my smallest expedition looks very different than that of a traditional large undertaking. I want to utilize periods of good weather without preparatory work to get up the mountain as high and fast as possible, then descend to return to the base camp as if fleeing. The important thing is not the preparation and not staying on the mountain, but lightning-fast action. This procedure corresponds to the business practices of disassembling auxiliary forces, decentralizing, downsizing, and reengineering processes.

Hunger for New Action

The more I identify with accomplishing a task that first exists as an idea and later packages itself as a concrete problem, the less pleased I am with the realization after achieving it. I always want to go one step farther. Not because I am dissatisfied with yesterday or with what was accomplished. Rather I hunger for new action. This hunger is my motivation for developing new ideas and starting new actions. Each idea that is realized tears a hole in my hopes for a short time. It does not slow me down. The hole can and must be filled with new ideas. One of these ideas can grow again, and solidify into a real utopia. Action follows.

While I, like Goethe, who placed the chain of recognition at the beginning of action, believe in the action-man inside us, I must place an action at the beginning of my chain of ideas, because the act eliminates all questions. All questions are answered through intensive activity.

I take up only real utopias in which I could fail. Border-crossing means risking doing something that you have never done. Being innovative means converting something into action that no one has ever succeeded in doing. You are a visionary border-crosser when you think of something that no one has ever thought of before. Action includes courage, energy, and conviction—above all, acting on your own self-understanding. Anyone who is oriented toward the self-understanding of others becomes, without noticing it, an imitator.

Project into the Future

I am at my best in the greatest challenges. My being this way is fed primarily by ideas, plans, and real utopias, less by what I have accomplished. I do not rest on my laurels. I also do not expect anything. I project my energies into the future, over and over again. What I have done belongs to my autobiography. I am also how I am, since I have this autobiography. I am packaged by the present, carried by tomorrow.

It is different with my image. My image lives from performances, also from the pictures that the media have drawn of me. My image is thus the imagination that others have of me. This picture seldom agrees with my personality. I am not my image.

Motivation for Innovation

Some ideas do not get supported because they are not clear enough, ripe enough, or good enough. Our supply of ideas comes out of our experience. The cycle is idea, action, idea. For example, when Hermann Buhl—then the most daring Austrian climber—set out in 1953 for Nanga Parbat, this 8,000-meter peak was the highest goal for all German-speaking mountain climbers. Through numerous attempts and tragedies, it had become the "German mountain of fate," equivalent to a desired but feared trophy. Although in his prime he was unsurpassed as a climber, Buhl was not a robust warhorse who could combat the stresses, the cold, and the oxygen-poor air. He was slight of build, had fine features, and was sensitive. Before the expedition, he was nervous as a racehorse. When he at long last reached the summit, it was only because he had identified himself with this peak, trained for months, and stayed possessed by his goal. On the last stretch, ascending alone, Buhl was able to pull out of himself more willpower, endurance, and willingness to suffer than any mountain-climber had ever done.

While he had the ability—acquired on more than 100 extreme climbing trips in the Alps—he also had the ability to wear himself out in his daydreams until he finally reached his goal, even though no one believed he could do it.

There have always been slight, small, and even sick border-crossers, climbers, explorers and travelers who pioneered new things. This shows that mental and spiritual abilities are needed more than raw strength. Even more so because a great deed depends on the strength of the vision that goes before it. Only when we think of another kind of humanity will we change ourselves. We need to reconsider our methods of "motivation" in this connection. An autonomous person who does what has to be done because it is also his idea will do his best. He thus does not have to be motivated (or manipulated by rewards, bribes, threats, punishments, or praise). As a creative actor, he creates meaning by realizing his daydreams.

Dissatisfied with the Status Quo

Since climbing Mount Everest without masks, I know how much more I can experience as an innovator. I must allow myself to fall back into my daydreams over and over again to get ahead. Anyone who considers the status quo has already lost it. So, be dissatisfied with the status quo. A realized vision leaves a hole in you for a short time. It is followed by a new idea and a new action. You become an action man, orientated toward your own self-understanding. Vision is not the same as image. Don't rest on your laurels. Adventure means always looking for something that hasn't been done yet. Courage to risk provokes new recognitions.

Creative Expression

For me, climbing—the conquest of the useless—represents a sport with possibilities for creative expression, not a religion or war game. So I do not plan and lead my expeditions in a military way. The true art of climbing is survival, and survival becomes most difficult when, having mastered what until then has been considered the epitome of achievement, you try to go one step, even one stage, further—to venture where no one has been before, and where hardly anyone wants to follow, or even understands what it is you are trying to do. It is there, in that unknown region, where sensations and experiences are found that are of far greater intensity than any from well-grazed lands.

Making a Game of Work

A person can do anything he wants. A healthy person, however, only wants what he can do. Creativity is making a game of work. Work starts with inertia; therefore, a loss in creativity. Being free of something is important, but be free to do something. Arranging logical thoughts is not my way. I question everything to cultivate creativity. Rules, dogmas, and bureaucracy are anti-creative. I don't accept anything blindly. Chaos is a better condition for creativity than order. Order does not correspond to reality. It is our ideal thinking. Creativity also grows in a climate of social, economic, scientific, and historical insights. I think in two halves, but I see things as a whole.

Goal-Directed Imagination

In the end, I am convinced that everything is possible that I want to do. The fact that I only want what I can do, provides me with healthy understanding at home. Without the power of goal-directed imagination, no border-crossing can be created or endured. A person is dead when he or she no longer requires his or her power of imagination, because all possibilities for experience are dead.

Interest in New Ideas

I have now become "the most successful mountainclimber," because I have climbed more than all others of my generation. If I only had a superficial interest in the new ideas, I would have developed neither the creativity nor the energy to risk 30 attempts on just the 8,000-meter peaks. If I now keep rolling the dice with persistence and impertinence, it is not because I can't give up the "kick," but primarily because I know that I find new combinations only by trying. Whenever I try to implement new ideas, there is a risk of failure. Border-crossers who were better than I have failed because they took the path to failure. Soon nothing occurred to them any more.

Creative Departures

As innovative explorers and mountain climbers, we understand that our "creative departures" will not change the world, but they do change our relationship to ourselves and to the world. We are creating for ourselves, outside of traditional work and organization, a playing field for our creative acts. Without the courage to get into our unknown, there is no innovation.

I hear every day the accusation that we border-crossers are fleeing reality. Perhaps that's true for some. I am sure, however, that I am not fleeing *from* anything or anyone. When I am underway, I am fleeing *to* something that is full of secrets and reality. My thoughts are not centered on nearby crises. In certain moments, I comprehend the whole, around me and in me. I recognize connections that can be observed only at a great distance. What has made me strong is this curiosity and the power of innovation that comes out of it. As I age, I see no danger of losing it. But time flies. For it is more difficult to do something new (innovation) than to find something new (creativity). The former is essentially dependent in border-crossing on body functions that decrease with increasing age.

Creative Teams

When I look back on three decades of mountain climbing and ice-crossings, I am amazed by how little courage and energy were used in accomplishing new ideas. There were "schools" in which there was fertilization of visions through deeds. Individual border-crossers started prodding each other to high performance, creating a push toward innovation and peak performance.

In the 1970s, it was a handful of Englishmen centered on Chris Bonington. In the 1980s, the Polish high-mountain climbers drove each other to more and more new border-crossings. Today, the Slovenian school dominates, although their master teachers are already dead. Norwegians have always been leaders as ice travelers, but the Englishmen challenged them and stimulated them to even more creativity.

Possibility Thinking

The wildernesses that are difficult to access—cliffs, mountains, deserts, ice seas—still permit us unique experiences. The return from the North Pole with one's own forces makes such an undertaking a challenge. This game possibility thus gives the trip an historical dimension: The North Pole, which by now can be visited by airplane and luxury liner, has still not been reached "by fair means"! Is the North Pole possible "by fair means"? Error-free thought is required —thinking through every possibility in advance, cleanly and in a disciplined manner in all aspects—but it is insufficient to answer this question. What today is dismissed as madness, tomorrow is already orthodox. I start by playing through all imaginable complications. Even this is not sufficient input for a solution. Endurance and ability are obviously the basis. Attempts are even more important—excluding errors by making errors, until the whole is possible. This "risk culture" costs time, money, and energy. At the same time, it requires combinations of possible solutions and personality development. Self-motivation cannot remain by the wayside.

Creative Inspiration

I try to look ahead 10 or 20 years. I am always planning for the distant future, but I keep the immediate goal before me much of the time. I must attract and decide on partners. It is always possible to find capable people if the project is important enough. The strength of conviction, inner momentum, and spirit also bring momentum to others. I have no worries that the ideas or the companions will leave me behind. Sometimes I doubt whether my skills and endurance will still be enough tomorrow for innovative border-crossings. At the same time, I hope that creativity will make a change of consciousness in my life one more time—to inspire me to vertical and horizontal border-crossings.

Creative Intelligence

When I describe myself as a border-crosser, game-player or semi-nomad, I don't mean that I live outside all civil laws and standards. All my "non-professions," however, stand for creativity. For this is tightly connected with risk, play, and travel. I experience "concrete intelligence"—the lightning-fast conversion of meaning impressions into a course of action—in contrast to the pure work of understanding—thinking in advance, remembering afterwards. My intelligence is associated with the ability to disconnect and get an overview.

Natural Feedback

As people become settled, they may become richer and well fed, but they tend to lose creativity. Nowhere can one get "filled up" as much as in the wilderness. Nature is always creative. It is always in motion, always new. When I give seminars, I often use the wilderness as a kind of "adventure playing field." This does not involve "outdoor training," but a personal "border experience" for the participant—a chance for him or her to shake off his or her "shell." Nature sets inescapable conditions. Its game rules cannot be manipulated, and they are infinitely diverse. Since feedback occurs faster in nature than in the world of work, I don't have to talk about leadership or team ability, self-management, or overcoming stress there. Through forced action, everyone experiences, immediately, the limits of his knowledge, planning, and actions. Rolling flexibility appears instead of the usual hierarchical behavior. Creative teams get the farthest here.

In the world of work, many of us are increasingly losing a connection with the result of our activity—we are losing the creative relationship with the end product. We sit for hours at the same desk, make the same things all year long: the same plans, the same calculations, the same movements. Everything goes routinely. In the wilderness, in contrast, there is the stimulus of experiencing something new, over and over again. A feeling of fulfillment follows.

I Do Not Work, I Play

I do not use the word "work" to describe what I do. Instead, I say that I am underway, I live, I am, I play. "Work" today usually starts with being sedentary. For thousands of years, people have both praised and damned work equally as the basis of supporting oneself. I praise what I do as "non-work." Even when I offer outdoor experiences and lectures to top people in business and politics, I am not working. I don't know whether this change of attitude can be applied in work or whether creativity is to be lost through work. Since I would like not to have to "work," I drive what I do with greater enthusiasm that many others. Enthusiasm is the fence over which the creative person has to jump, over and over again. Computers are wonderful work tools, but less wonderful creativity tools. Computability stops where probability starts. And in life, everything is probability. And probability and possibility are best addressed through play.

Freedom for Something

If I use the concept of "being free," I mean not only freedom *from* something but also freedom *for* something. To be creative, I must first be able to question status quo, rules, dogmas, and bureaucracy. Everything that is ordinary, running properly, and fixed in writing is anti-creative! Creativity means risking, playing, and rolling the dice. To come up with new ideas, I must not assume anything as given. I must be open to the unexpected, ready also to lose. The basic requirements for a creative life are curiosity, action, and failure. It is not the one who jumps over borders who is crazy, but the one who denies them.

The Creative Life

I am no longer a 20-year-old beginning climber, but my creative energy still seeks for itself an outlet, an existence, an expression, a place, a reserve, and a playing field. I would not exchange my life for anyone else's life, even though I know that I cannot possess anything that I have experienced or achieved, except my memories. I am free to look to the future. Even yesterday's experience and good will are not enough. While it is true that life is full of failures and tensions, these are not powerful enough to threaten or defeat me. The radical nature of my life as a border-crosser shows that we can prevail—we can even use pure accidents to our advantage. I am still programmed for the future. Even when I now play with turning off the basic necessities of life—oxygen, light, heat, water, fire, land—optimism remains my basic attitude (in spite of self-criticism). My border-crossings are experiments for myself, not for society, and so I pose no danger to this diligent, frightened, unimaginative world. I fill my daydreams with myths and legends. In this way, a grand idea comes out. This lets me gain energy. Although I know rationally that every new idea is as useless as the one before, I develop a pronounced self-under-standing for it—until it is realized or fulfilled.

Watch Your Language

Not only must we border-crossers do away with military language—and get away from the gestures of the con-querors—we must also get away from the planning and strat-egy that corresponds to military metaphors. Autonomous action, situational creativity, and courage to change are the bases for a possible tomorrow. In a language that is full of mil-itary metaphors—"winning the summit," "rallying the troops," "attacking the summit," and "assaulting the sum-mit," we will not bring the game-like nature of our actions or the play-like nature of our minds to bear. With a new spirit, we also need a new language.

Divine Creativity

Creativity, our "divine characteristic," is the strongest power of the human spirit. The "limitlessness" of the human spirit is unused without limits. It involves comprehending new dimensions through our consciousness. To implement creativity and to create meaning is more in demand today than anything else. We want and need to make human existence more peaceful and livable. Our lives here on earth are tran-sient. Every individual dies. The only question to be asked is "How we will shape our time?" The mass of humanity on this earth makes this recognition relative. We have become too many. Everything gets out of balance. But we are still always maximizing profit. The free-market economy must lead inescapably to catastrophe, if nature is not taken into consid-eration in the addition and subtraction to increase the gross social product. As long as the group is small, it is often true that the total energy is greater than the sum of the individual energies. Transferred to humanity, the principle of synergy no longer applies, except in relation to their destructive potential. So, it is necessary that mountains be moved by each of us. The individual must rethink things and find his way out of the lethargy of "everyone is doing it" to make life more bearable for everyone—even if only for a limited time.

Creativity Tricks

My creativity "tricks" include: Pay attention to your inside! Learn to dream! Under a free sky, thoughts also go farther! Visualize real utopia (when half asleep)! Wake up and arise ready to learn! Take a cold shower! You think more clearly when walking! Avoid thinking in order to clarify thoughts! Learn through direct experience and consequences! Two things cannot have priority at the same time! Imagine planned changes in a relaxed state! There are no limits, if we eliminate them! Our lives are shaped more by our consciousness and less by circumstances! **MM**

* * *

Application and Action:

Application: In this season of innovation, we should find many lessons to apply to our lives and our leadership. For example, we might assess the quality and quantity of our creative ideas, the game rules we follow, and the strategies we pursue. We might ask if our minds and bodies are fed as much by ideas and utopias as they are by food and drink. Messner reminds us that good ideas—and those who generate them—need support to survive. He invites us to feed our fantasies and give expression to our best and brightest ideas.

Action: Express your creativity in some activity that you find rewarding. Seek the new spirit and new language of "play" that is part of the creative life. **AA**

Chapter 19

Path-breaking and Pioneering

Although most people stay on the "beaten path," Messner prefers to break new paths and pioneer new projects, taking it one step at a time. The real pioneers experiment with what's possible and push the limits, sometimes alone, along new paths. The bold explorer, Sir Ernest Shackleton, failed in most of his projects, but he succeeded in his pioneering. Messner's ice crossings at the poles serve as examples of goals directed by imagination. The future orientation keeps us looking forward to the next adventure. Even after "failures," Messner dreams about the next step—daydreams where he can go his own way. The lessons for life and business, again, are many. The challenge is to find new ideas at the edge of our ability and "load capacity." We need creative pauses that give life to new adventures.

✳   ✳   ✳

Planning vs. Serendipity

Human nature and the cosmos control my bio-rhythms. For the rest I can anticipate nothing and everything. My planned solo climb is like life, a mystery—unpredictable, risky, often dependent on chance, and thereby illogical. Any attempt to preplan it would be madness. An Everest solo climb is not an arithmetical exercise. Luckily for me I believe in human instincts. If in nature a man confronts only two possibilities—death or survival—he does the right thing. Only I cannot rehearse it—there is only the real thing.

One Step at a Time

These steps forward I take in mountaineering must never be taken two at a time. If you want to push out limits, you have to do it slowly, stealthily, bit by bit, step by step. If you go too fast, and try to leap-frog stages, sooner or later you will stumble and fall. And in climbing, a fall can mean death.

Real Pioneers

In the uneasy fog of self-aggrandizement, the mountain climber, from one generation to the next, fancies himself superior to those who have gone before, and especially so to the ordinary man-in-the-street. Thus, he will follow blindly, nose to tail with others, along well trodden paths—oblivious to the fact that these trails were discovered a century before by an illustrious company of lone travelers who journeyed without maps or other aids, and without the benefit of experience. These pioneers with none of today's advantages were propelled with the self-confidence that characterizes the Victorian period. Besides, mountains were there to be conquered. We, the limit-pushers of that day, experimented without national banners or oxygen masks. First on the difficult faces, then with traverses, and then in ever-smaller groups. The "how" had become more important to us than the "how many" or "at any price." In this way I was able to discover and develop my own style.

Bold Ideas, New Paths

Does it sound improbable for a nonprofessional explorer, one who no longer knows where he is, who is confronted with his limits, to stand at the edge of an abyss, and flirt with new, perhaps still bolder ideas? It is often this way with me. Instead of thinking about giving up my expeditions, I think up new ones, again and again. And I am not the only adventurer who reacts this way. Thus we see the question that predominantly resurfaces when we fail: Shouldn't we continuously discover our world anew? One who goes alone on an old path practices a new style. A new path in going alone is a double step forward. A dangerous path in going alone is the best of all. I'm never satisfied. I still face the challenge of going one step farther. My efforts toward peak performances (excellent activities) cannot be satisfied. Higher, longer, and faster are not so important in this. The "what" and "how" count more.

Sir Ernest Shackleton

Sir Ernest Shackleton, in my view the boldest ice explorer of the 20th century, always came to new ideas, because he failed again and again. None of his projects saw success to the end. He always had to turn back, but his experiences were always positive. They lent wings to ever bolder steps to cross more borders. At the beginning of the 20th century, Shackleton, as well as Scott and Dr. Wilson, mushed across the Ross Ice Shelf toward the South Pole. They reached a point shortly before the gateway. They suspected it was the beginning of the Antarctic high plateau. On the return trip, they experienced some dramatic moments.

Even though Scott Shackleton pushed for a further expedition "too weakly," this self-willed Irishman began his own attempt: the journey to the South Pole on foot. With three friends, he ascended the gateway and the Beardmore Glacier, then advanced far inside the Antarctic. They almost reached the South Pole. Realizing that time, fuel, and food were not sufficient to reach the South Pole, Shackleton turned around. The retreat became a race with death. Nevertheless, Shackleton came back in 1914. He wanted to cross the Antarctic from the Weddel sea, over the South Pole. In the meantime, Amundsen and Scott had already reached it. Shackleton wanted to go a step further. He failed at the very beginning of this expedition, but it took years to rescue himself. Shackleton and his crew went through everything humans can possibly endure. The only reasons they came home at the very end—even though their ship, named "Endurance," had been crushed by icebergs like a nutshell—

were because of Schackleton's talent as a leader and the unity of the crew, which had grown with necessity.

Shackleton still hadn't done enough. In the 1920s he traveled to the Antarctic a fourth time. He died of heart failure at the edge of the ice, without being able to undertake a further attempt to penetrate inside the "seventh continent."

New Successes

Climbing at the right moment leads to new successes, as illustrated in three examples from the world of alpine climbing. First, Luis Trenker, the famous film maker and storyteller, was a good climber before the first World War. After a period as a front-line soldier, then the subsequent architecture study, he once again began climbing mountains. But then he became a film maker. Throughout his filming he continued to climb, but through the 1930s he transferred all his energy for the film medium: as an actor, script writer, producer, and director. Climbing in and of itself was no longer important to him, but the representation of mountain climbing was.

Second, Italian Walter Bonatti, surely the most successful mountain climber between 1955 and 1965, gave up extreme mountain climbing after his solo climb of the Matterhorn's north face in the winter of 1965. He became a photojournalist, and produced stories for renowned magazines with great success.

Third, Martin Schliessler was one of the best mountain climbers in Germany in the 1950s, and later he transferred to the film business and produced exciting documentary films as a cameraman and producer. He is also an artist. He always changes from one activity to another. His occupations are a calling to him: sculptor, documentary film maker, adventurer.

Ghost Trains in the Head

On the trip home from Antarctica in February 1990, I realize that I also want to go to the North Pole. It is, like the South Pole, only a fictitious point, invented by the human spirit. It can't be seen like the summit of a mountain, can't be grasped like a handle, but it can be strived for and achieved like any goal in the head. It can be found by means of the stars, natural or artificial, as one point out of a million on a layer of ice two-meters thick, on which the Northern Polar Sea drifts. So, I start a study of past Arctic trips. The expeditions of early arctic explorers and the dreams associated with them became for me like a trip in a ghost train through the pack ice.

Imagine the Possibilities

Exploration always involves self-understanding—where are my weaknesses, my "open windows," my psychological and physical reserves? Nevertheless, practical questions stand in the foreground. A "blind leap" into pack ice would be stupid. To respond to all logistical questions, I feed my fantasies with more new stories. Starting from fleeting probabilities—nothing is more uncertain in its chaos than drifting ice in the polar sea—I can imagine myself, the craziest border-crosser, there. I start to imagine a dozen possibilities for achieving this goal. However, by listening to my inner voice, I realize that if I want to preserve the quality of the trip, only a handful of possibilities remain. My task is to go without motors of any kind, with the least possible help from the outside, and with the return trip the most important part of the requirements. Now it is necessary to find partners for this real utopia. Then, visions will be contributed from several people, and the chance of realization increases. The first thing for me is an attempt. Without risking an attempt, I cannot come to the combination of solutions.

Simulated vs. Situational Experience

At indoor training events (lectures on border-crossings, for example), if someone says that "everyone is climbing his own Mount Everest" or that "mistakes are fatal on a solo climb," these remain empty phrases—even embarrassing, when the solo climber who appears can still tell about his fall. Such talks create caution, but no stimulation, inhalation, or deep breathing. Good mottoes—even if based on valid ideas—are of less value than real experiences, real situations, real responsibility. Authentic experiences of a serious nature—when told—have mostly only informational value to other border-crossers. For outsiders, they may have conversational value, no more. Nothing is easier for an "adventurer" than to convert his non-adventurer listeners' hunger for experiences into wonderment. But the ability to make wise judgments only arises when it is required. This is true in every field.

Pioneering New Paths

In adventure, players have always pioneered new things. Sir Edmund Hillary, for example, the first climber of Mount Everest, was for 40 years not envisioned for the climb to the summit. When, however, earlier attempts to reach the summit from the south summit to the north summit failed, Hillary was ready to risk an attempt. In the Sherpa Tenzing, who was possessed by success and had repeatedly failed to reach the summit of Everest, he had the best possible partner. They both not only wanted success, because their predecessors had accumulated the necessary stock of experiences for that, they were ready to risk playing the game in another combination. Hillary and Tenzing bivouacked in an intermediate camp at 8,500 meters (26,247 feet), before going to the top. No one had ever spent the night at such a great altitude. But because Hillary and Tenzing found this combination, they were able to accomplish the feat.

Amundsen, with his little ship, had success because he was creative. His mini-expedition accomplished what gigantic undertakings had paid for with tragedy. Although Nansen, the most creative of all Arctic travellers, did not reach the North Pole, he did march around the 85th degree of latitude with Johannsen and survived to return to Franz-Joseph Land. The "Fram" trip seems to be unbeatable in drama and difficulty. ("Fram" was Nansen's ship, the name means "Forward" in translation.) Nansen was often for the unthinkable. In the chaos of drifting ice masses, he found the creativity for the ship and the group to survive the worst dangers. Day after day, month after month, year after year. As crazy as it may sound, chaos is the best condition for creativity as order. Order is only our dream thought, even when classical physics fools us with order. It is superficial, thought up by ourselves. No limits can be placed on thinking.

Laws of Nature

Creativity grows in us with insight into the "Laws of Nature," with experiences and impressions of a social, economic, and historical kind. Even more so when we are thrown into chaos—from outside or from within ourselves—that hides the world under a varnish of prejudices. How fast you learn to see, think, and sense globally when you are pushed to your limits in the wilderness! Thought and action become one, as if the two halves of your brain start to think in synchrony. Everything that is perceived on several levels is also known on several levels.

I want to have the chance—through membership in a universal, democratic welfare society—to be delivered into the unknown: with daily risks, the wilderness before me, the obligation to prove things to myself, because I want to experience life on many levels. I would not want to sink to being the most frightened herd or food animal. I measure the quality of my life according to the quality of the requirements, not the quantity of the material comforts.

The Next Adventure

After failures, I dream about the next adventure—now already taking form in my subconscious mind. For example, in summer 1995, four months after the early Arctic crossing, I fractured the right femur bone in a fall and was unable to walk for months. But I did not give up on the North Pole idea. Several surgical operations were needed before I could even walk again. And then I faced months of training and rehabilitation to regain my endurance. But even when I am handicapped in walking, I don't want to give up on myself. Adjusting to completely new situations in life—illness, poverty, age, injury—is part of those abilities that grow by dealing with chaos. Naturally, no one gets over such problems by playing games. Still, there are always alternatives for everyone with faith in the future. To look for this alternative—and even to start to act on it—is the creative art in this life.

Imagine the Next Step

I hope that I will never deceive myself in this life quest. I am ready and willing to ask more experienced people for advice in finding my new fields or tasks. There are not only mountains to climb but also deserts and ice fields to cross. I can imagine a series of activities for myself, in which I place meaning, in which I find pleasure, and in which I can use my whole personality, independent of what I am motivated by, to bring myself, even without an external stimulation, to accomplish something. So, while I am, for the first time busy with stepping out of the world of the border-crossers, I stay with my plans. First of all, I want to be completely healthy again.

At the same time, slowly another daydream is maturing: to stand once in a desert—with only a backpack, without a precise map, not knowing where I am—and somehow getting through. This maximum chance is still possible for me as "an invalid." Such asceticism is possible, however, only on solid ground, not at the North Pole, which I want to reach first.

Go Your Own Way

Just as my mountain-climbing was different from that of the grail-keeping of Alpinism, I also want to go my way as a border-crosser. I am not bound to anyone by unquestioned loyalty, and I want to be a thorn in the eye of the Pharisees. So I will continue to defend my acts through my dreams, my existence, and my acts. I am a living contradiction to current institutions. As I age in life, I do not want just to be looking back at my biography. I will go further. I must. If I am dissatisfied, I will become ill and lose my strength and even my creative power. In my quest of the "useless," I am more alive. Reaching the North Pole, where I could just as well fail for a second time, means more to me now than the climbing of all 8,000-meter peaks combined. In this way, I live more for today and for tomorrow, and less from yesterday.

Lessons for Business

What do we border-crossers have to give to business or politics? We have only our experiences. A person who accomplishes much in his field of activity may find it interesting to listen to experiences from border-crossers of another kind. How far these lessons can be implemented, however, remains doubtful. They remain second-hand results, as long as the "students" are not taken along on the adventure. On the other hand, stepping out to get into or around something temporarily does them good. Personally, I hate sterile debates about ideology, the many recommendations about improving the world. I believe the consciousness of the individual must change first; otherwise, any undertaking is a waste of time, or squandered strength.

Some mountain-climbers, adventurers, and seafarers get drawn into management training. Naturally, a manager at IBM or the branch director of bank cannot climb Mount Everest with me or go to the North Pole, but he can find new ideas at the edge of his ability to bear a load—on smaller mountains, in quiet places, or in the ideal case, in small groups. A couple of days outside his field of work are sufficient to create a base under his feet for going forward, to open his eyes. Each of us needs creative pauses. Alpinist John Amatt trained managers for decades in a concept he called "Adventure Attitude." I, too, believe that casting people into an adventure in nature breaks down their fears and uncertainties—fear of living, of loneliness, disorientation, and death.

Backs to the Wall

The competitive situation today forces many of us toward an attitude that is similar to the attitude of a border-crosser when he stands with his back to the wall. In a sense, we are all standing with our backs to the wall. At the beginning of the 20th century in the western industrial countries, the social problem awaited a solution. Now at the beginning of the 21st century, the ecological problem awaits a solution. We need visionary leaders to get us out of its cul-de-sacs.

The path to from the "infinite beginning" to "infinite meaning" seems, when considered from the viewpoint of history, to have been a short distance. The slower the risks grow and the more they affect people, the blinder we are to them. The resources on this earth are finite. Even humanity is finite. Only the spirit is infinite. **MM**

* * *

Application and Action:

Application: In this chapter, Messner suggests the applications for individuals, teams, and organizations in need of some new ideas, approaches, and projects. With our backs to the wall, we need visionary leaders who can get us out of mental ruts and procedural cul-de-sacs. Since the spirit is infinite, we can create a path from infinite beginnings to infinite meaning.

Action: Put one of your ideas or daydreams for path-breaking, border-crossing, and pioneering into action in your life or profession. **AA**

Chapter 20
Personal Qualities

In this chapter, Messner outlines some of the personal qualities needed not only by mountaineers, but also by pioneers in every walk of life. His is a character-based model of success. His desired qualities include humility, love, stamina, enthusiasm, discipline, passion, responsibility, courage, and wisdom. Those who seek wealth and fame along an easy path may find their wealth to be slippery and their fame fleeting. Character is the composition of real success. All other avenues to success are but shortcuts, even detours, and may lead to disaster. Much of what we hope to be in life—the personal qualities and characteristics we covet—we can only achieve by doing, by actively pursuing a life dream. In a passive or reactive life, the qualities of greatness cannot grow. Wise people are active people.

* * *

Qualities of Character

Climbing's highest qualities of self-sufficiency, level-headedness under exposure, team spirit, and learning from failure have become corrupted into farce over the space of one decade, during which the great mountains have been denigrated into consumables. The consequences are disastrous: trashed mountains, an increasing number of disasters, and diminished creativity among high-altitude mountaineers. Where once, among insiders, recognition was granted only to those who tackled the hardest routes with a minimum of equipment, this mutated during the 1990s, when the two ordinary routes on Everest were turned into mountaineering's prime goals. In the mass media, that is almost all they talk about. It is as if the highest mountains on earth serve better than anything else—better even than character and contribution—as a springboard to fame.

Humility—Shadow of Self

When I was descending from the summit of K2, I saw out to the east the shadow of K2 cast across the mountain ranges beneath me. And on the very top of this shadow I could make out a tiny dot. Was it me? Some years later, my daughter Layla asked me why I had not waited for the mountain to "go to sleep" before climbing to the top. Her words immediately conjured in my imagination the silhouette of K2. She continued, "Yes, then, when the mountain got up in the morning, you would have been on top." How simple it would be if mountains really slept, or if we were blessed with the ability to project ourselves to the top of 8,000ers on the wings of our imagination. With such unearthly powers, we would certainly reach the highest points without the effort and danger it costs us now. But so long as I am unable to step right outside this physical world, I find the greatest adventures do not take place in the head—that is only where they begin.

Mountains are so elemental that man does not have the right nor the need to subdue them with technology. Only the man who chooses his tools with humility can experience natural harmony. No one of us sets out to be the best. There's no such thing as the best mountaineer in the world, nor the fastest, nor the most outstanding. These are attitudes invented by journalists or publishers. An adolescent rock climber may occasionally promote himself with superlatives like these, because he knows that in big mountaineering there are no gold medals or world titles.

Personality alone is what counts, along with the capacity for survival in increasingly more demanding situations.

Mountaineering is not measurable in points and seconds—its only calculable absolutes are metric heights and grades of difficulty.

Loving—Hungry for Love

The end of an expedition does not just mean being able to relax your guard and feel safer. It also means loving and belonging. My need to give myself completely to someone else, my partner, was never stronger than after coming down off a big mountain. Danger past makes me crave new "borderline" experiences, but I am also hungry for love and for death. Death is preceded by many "little deaths." Perhaps that explains my heightened need for love before and after experiences at the edge of human existence, explains why my longing for human contact is so great. It is perhaps for this reason that the nomads love their homeland more than stationary citizens, because they must be forever discovering it anew. Or do most citizens understand by "home" primarily only possessions—things that wind and time decay like autumn leaves? My roots lie deeper, in the stones.

Stamina—Essential for Success

When I think how tired I have been after climbing any one 8,000-meter mountain, I cannot today imagine how we managed to do two together without stopping. In 1970 after Nanga Parbat I was close to death. In 1972 after Manaslu, I was sad and burnt out. In 1975 after Hidden Peak, my third 8,000er, I was plagued by hallucinations. Now after the descent from Gasherbrum II, I still felt quite fresh. This certainly had something to do with the fact that we were committed to a double traverse from the start. We knew that the essential stamina would only come to us after the first 8,000er.

Energy and Enthusiasm

No one had climbed two 8,000ers in one season before 1986, but we were not the first to try it. What caused the others to fail? We wanted to do it more! We wanted to climb two of the five highest mountains in the world in the space of two months, without using artificial oxygen. What we needed above all for this daring venture was energy, the sort of energy that only springs from enthusiasm.

This enthusiasm of mine for things makes me seem scurrilous and crazy to many outsiders, but it also makes me immune to self-satisfaction and self-sufficiency. It allows me to be alert, find original solutions, and do things that are important only to me. I take my adventures so seriously that I even subject myself to what I get into. Being wholly into something has nothing to do with representing myself. It is the forced consequence of being one with my action: conception, internalization, self-development. In this there arises a state of spiritual and physical excitement. Target, arrow, and archer can become one in spirit. Being a bow and arrow simultaneously is only possible for one who has first been a target.

Climbing mountains requires a great deal of energy. Only we recover energy, almost in the same amount we expend. Every time I have thought back on the 8,000-meter climbs, I have had the certainty that I have discovered myself again. I have felt stronger than ever. Sometimes it was as if I had been reborn. As long as one travels as an amateur, combining his "border adventure" with vacation, he will never experience this recovery of energy, this rebirth. The same applies to the millionaire. The recovery of energy and enthusiasm comes honestly to the border-crosser, who is always pushing forward.

Discipline and Determination

I had been much more resolved in my mind on my first attempt of Everest—more resolved not only in my attitude to chance it, but also in my determination to carry on until I reached the end of my resources. But then, also, I was far more strongly convinced that it could be done. Now I am frightened, so frightened I can't rest. I toss from side to side, worrying my head with questions I cannot answer, questions no one can answer, not even someone who has climbed Everest before. I often ask myself where I find the strength and motivation to keep setting out afresh, after success and after failure. It isn't ambition. It is purely discipline—mental, physical, and spiritual discipline—that makes any extended achievement possible.

Strength of Passion

Strength grows slowly in the heart of a lone wolf. It must grow, until it bursts upon me. It must grow like love. If this passionate strength fails, all action becomes calculation, determination, only a matter of judgment. And what has reason to put up against the deadly risk of avalanches, crevasses, and exhaustion? Too little. Firmness, especially severity towards oneself, cannot be learned overnight. Concentrated energy stores up only in the long period of waiting and hoping. Only when an idea becomes a passion does it become independent and seek an outlet. But all passion fizzles away without willpower, and this willpower must become perseverance, a toughness not paralyzed by altitude.

Self-Responsibility

It is so difficult to take upon yourself all responsibility, not only for your actions, but also for your thoughts and emotions, especially if your whole body is desperate through exertion. Perhaps because of the risks I freely enter into, I cannot entrust myself wholly to God or anyone else. To what then? During the ascent I am like a walking corpse. What holds me upright is the world around me: air, sky, earth, the clouds—the experience of proceeding one step at a time over terrain that demands my whole attention. That I can stand, that I can proceed, gives me energy to think ahead, to want to go ahead. At least as important as "success" is joy at one's own skill. High-altitude climbing requires a whole range of proficiencies, knowledge, and inventiveness. The higher you go, the more you yourself become the problem. Ability to solve problems of this sort is what makes a good climber.

Courage

Courage should not be viewed separately from fear. It is the flip side of fear. Courage has nothing to do with fearlessness in the face of death or love or risk. It grows in me out of knowing that I can play my game according to my rules.

Wisdom

My life goal—in the long run—is to become wise. I want to be neither a rich man nor a successful, obscure old man (should I reach old age)—I want to be a wise old man. To be wise means to have experiences. It means perspective, tolerance, generosity. To understand and know are much, but wisdom is more: with all purpose, with heart, with understanding to know how limited we are. Above all, to be wise means to discern and acknowledge human boundaries. This is more important than discerning and acknowledging human possibilities. Human limitation becomes ultimately evident through failure. It is like flying backwards. And it makes us human. Being wise does not mean being passive. Wise people are active people. **MM**

*　　*　　*

Application and Action:

Application: With a spirit of humility, face the mountain in front of you. Devise a path for getting from where you are now to the desired destination and begin to exercise the qualities of character mentioned in this chapter. As you do, these admirable qualities will grow and give you greater capacity for the climb.

Action: Pursue a course of action that demands the exercise of your best qualities of character. **AA**

A Rare Human Being

by Henri Sigayret, climber of Annapurna,
expedition leader

In 1984 when my companions and I attempted a new route on the north side of Annapurna—right of the Main Summit—a tent in which two of my friends were sleeping was swept away by an avalanche. We were never able to find them.

Since 1950 many expeditions have attempted Annapurna. A dozen variations and new routes have been opened up. Only the Northwest Flank remained unclimbed, and this promised to be a formidable proposition, even for the dauntless. It is a receptacle for avalanches, and very steep, with barriers of crumbling rock and over-hanging ice. A multi-crevassed glacier guards the foot of the mountain, making passage onto the face a problem in itself.

In 1985 Reinhold Messner wanted to climb Annapurna. He could have climbed the normal route on the North Face in his usual fast manner and easily "bagged" his 11th 8,000er. But he refused the sure and simple option of climbing the mountain in two or three days, turning his attention instead to the Northwest Face. There, with resolution and in exemplary expedition style, he selected a direct and complex route. Two camps were established; and after two further bivouacs, he reached the top.

At that time, there were very few Alpinists who could stand head and shoulders above the rest. They were all men who, confronted with natural problems, could come up with interesting solutions. Rarer, were those climbers who, foreswearing the obvious, engineered original and elegant solutions to their problems. These were the innovators, the forerunners of later trends. Often criticized by the mediocre or jealous, they accomplished what others have considered impossible and did so with a certain brilliance and facility. Reinhold Messner is such a one.

Rarer still, are those Alpinists who stand out from their contemporaries in such divergent disciplines as free-climbing, ice-climbing, and Himalayan mountaineering. Reinhold Messner is such a one. And how seldom do you find Alpinists whose passion—the driving force for pioneering feats of vision—has not waned over long periods of activity! Reinhold Messner is such a one. Finally, singular phenomena indeed are those Alpinists who have preserved their experiences faithfully in work and picture, and thus enabled others to share them. Such a one, too, is Reinhold Messner. Reinhold Messner is truly the most extraordinary mountaineer. But it is an inadequate definition. Above all, he is a man of stature, an extraordinary human being.

A Splendid Organizer

by Max Eiselin, leader of the
Dhaulagiri Expedition, 1960

That Reinhold Messner survived on Dhaulagiri, too, must go down as one of his greatest experiences. Naturally a hefty chunk of luck comes into play. I remember particularly the first time he attempted this mountain, when, having taken on the exceedingly dangerous South Face, he made a dramatic yet unscathed retreat from it. Messner's ability to turn back on a mountain was put to the test again on his second Dhaulagiri attempt seven years later, when, in the face of extreme bad weather, he favored a timely withdrawal to struggling on at all costs. This was no easy decision with all that lost time and expense of preparation, the bureaucratic formalities, and the long march-in. But Reinhold Messner is such a shrewd tactician and husbandman, he acts as if he does not find it unrewarding to struggle for weeks on end against the superior might of the unbridled elements, burning himself out from the effects of storms and altitude. He possesses a maturity that enables him to wait patiently, and then at a precise moment to "strike" with elegant speed. He owes his eventual summit success on the third attempt to his multifaceted ability. Clearly, he is not exaggerating when he remarks that it was "a wonder" they were not struck by lightening on the exposed summit ridge. Yet, to this "wonder" his own survival instincts made a contribution, as did the mountaineer's luck—without which, in Alpinism, simply nothing goes— and his speed of movement, born of his extraordinary condition.

Reinhold Messner has always had the inner calm and assuredness to know exactly when the time was right to return to the scene of a retreat—even after years. He is not only a brilliant climber, but a splendid organizer. He applies the same diligence and rigid discipline that have made his hardest mountaineering deeds possible, to equally hard commercial and publicity work, and has managed to create the necessary foundations for his expedition activity, which so many people envy. Reinhold Messner need feel no shame in attaining his economic goals. It has brought him nothing; hard work and iron discipline alone have led to his well-earned success.

Section V

*　*　*

Management and Leadership

As we move from solo adventures to tandem climbs to small teams to organizing and leading major expeditions, we need to develop and employ different skill sets and mindsets. Messner subscribes to the model of the "practical idealist." His dreams may begin in the clouds, but they soon have funding and a foundation under them. Hence, he has mastered the skills of management and leadership, including the disciplines of financing, logistics, strategy, and planning and all aspects of teamwork. These basic skills have afforded Messner—as they do all masters of management—many opportunities to pursue projects, finish climbs, build on past success, finance expeditions, and achieve goals. His sponsors and other "stakeholders" have shared in his success. In working with team members, he values differences and seeks for a positive synergy that allows the whole to be greater than the sum of the parts.

Chapter 21

Financing and Logistics

Once the dream is fixed, Messner becomes a manager whose main tasks are financing and logistics—finding money and organizing all the moving parts of the expedition. It takes a lot of work to start and keep a project in motion and on target. The master of budgets, schedules, and supply trains, Messner keeps the momentum going toward goal. Realization is converting an idea into action by following a correct sequence of events: idea and action become one; thought and deed are identical. Marketing makes the magic all possible. Return on investment is the bottom line, and the capital of credibility is all that matters in the end. The trick in any trade is to translate the dream into financial gain, and the best way to do that is to invest in what you do best and seek connections to the market.

*　*　*

Mastering Various Activities

The most varied abilities are a requirement for keeping border-crossing activities in motion: financing, teamwork, finding and testing equipment, climbing ability, training, endurance, evaluation in the form of lectures, books, reports, and documentary films. Finding out what suits me and at which stage in life. I am an idea creator, strategist, and decision maker in one person. I am never openly a know-how trigger. Specialist knowledge and generalist knowledge can be provided. Partners must also be self-aware. We set standards for tasks. We coordinate unimportant and important things. In the end, I am responsible myself if something doesn't work. The adventure starts exclusively in the head. Realization is converting an idea into action. The art in this is the correct sequence. Idea and action become one; thought and deed are identical. I understand action as an open learning process, not as heroism. Self-understanding is the result.

The Money Side

Every border-crossing involves earning money intensively. How can I accomplish two or three expeditions a year if I have not financed them previously? The principle of self-sufficiency—the border crossing feeds the border-crosser—is part of my self-understanding. I live financially from the "byproducts" of what I do. I have full understanding for all those who cannot bring my personality as a money-earner into harmony with my personality as a border-crosser. But I am not composed of two halves. It only appears so. Together, they form my personality.

The Money Cycle

The money cycle of a border-crosser only becomes obvious when one is a border-crosser. If I have become more successful than another person in my playing field, this is because I have learned how to sell my "byproducts" (stories, lectures, experiences, knowledge) better than others. As a lecturer, author of books, and advertiser, I am now capable of earning enough money within a few months that I can be on the road for the rest of the year without having to think about money. This, in turn, is a requirement for external success, and yet money is not my motive. Anyone on Mount Everest who is thinking only about making a financial profit will not get far.

Cost-Benefit Analysis

I have my back free for border-crossers who, though they may fail, can also guarantee an increased market value if they succeed—so I can stand on my own feet and return for additional expeditions. For 10 years, I have tried to get myself out of the hectic cycle of financing expeditions in advance by promises for the future and evaluation as debt-settlement. My rhythm more recently has been—financing on the free market, execution, evaluation. The critical step in going from the first system to the second came with the small expedition. I suddenly had the financial key in my head for gaining much money with little money. The better strategy also resulted in a more favorable cost-benefit calculation. Although I had not imagined this analysis, it was strikingly clear afterward.

All expeditions must stand against all cost calculations or benefit analyses. They cost time, money, and energy. Each trip must pay for itself; otherwise, I cannot live as a border-crosser for long. I have, therefore, learned to take note of my image and to evaluate my trips.

Marketing Professionals

Marketing is an integral part of an expedition. Anyone who does not admit to being a "full-time border-crosser," deceives himself or his club, his fans, or his sponsors. In marketing too, it can be seen who is a pro and who is not. This does mean that I will go on an expedition only if it promises to become a success financially. It must only be possible to finance the expedition. It doesn't have to make a profit. Only afterwards, with my greater experience, greater charisma, can I bring stories, pictures, and my reliability to the market.

Invest in Your Dreams

I have adapted my financial proceeds to my private market rules. I do not invest my money in "financial"companies; I invest them in my dreams—whether my mountain, my farmyard, or my border crossings. In this, I seek to keep the costs as low as possible, and I measure the benefits in term of quality of life. This is what my investments look like. I will only be able to finance a border-crossing; it must not discard anything. It is self-sufficient. One who plays out of suffering is neither a gladiator nor an actor. He plays unconditionally, even when he goes down, but never unselfishly. Profit-and-loss calculations are for me not in units of money. To realize my dreams, I sell a portion of my time and my energy. In this way, I have the rest of the time for myself. I also try in this to stay true to myself. Currying favor does not appeal to me.

Capital of Credibility

How long it has taken me to find the self-understanding as an advertiser so that today this is part of my financial success! With this, I know precisely with each advertisement that is run in connection with my personality, my self-worth suffers. Every dollar that I invest as an advertiser costs credit with my readers, listeners, and fans. My capital of credibility can be refilled only with new deeds, successes, and experiences. It is important to decide for myself how much freedom I give up to acquire the necessary money. I try never to give up my entire capital, but to live from the interest on my capital.

Ethics of Sponsoring

In art and in sports, sponsoring has become an obvious fact of life. Just as most magazines, newspapers, and television programs could not be produced if there were no advertising, it is the same with concerts, sports events, and border-crossings. But sponsoring has its limits. Since I am a non-smoker, I have never accepted cigarette advertising in any form. A Camel trophy and Marlboro freedom are horrors to me, although I have received high offers in connection with tobacco products. I will be more cautious in the future in connection with alcohol. I don't seek for sponsors myself. I decide on similar questions whether I am interested in accepting cooperation with a particular company or a certain product. At the beginning of my advertising time, I made mistakes. I used every dollar to realize dreams that I could realize only in the years of my youth, and I "sold" myself forever.

Public or Private

Researchers and mountain-climbers, who were active in the early 1900s through the 1950s in climbing the highest mountains in the world for the first time, were often supported by state treasuries, clubs, and sponsors. This time is past, happily. It is not proper to spend public money on what can be pursued as one's personal daydream. While public sources of money have mostly disappeared, we have learned to find other solutions. We finance almost all of our expeditions from the free market. There is a lecture and book market on the subject of border crossing. Anyone who has learned to minimize costs and maximize benefits will go far. When I do a series of lectures in parallel with the appearance of a book, I can sell both better. In 1982, climbing an 8,000-meter peak was no longer interesting enough for the general public. A combination of several 8,000-meter peaks was favorable for financing and could be exploited, as my success at that time has shown. The law of comparative costs applies to me just as to the economy.

Invest in What You Do Best

The trip itself is like a piece of life outside the market. It follows other laws: giving meaning, motivation, and success. In difficult undertakings, I do as much as possible myself: in preparations, financing, and naturally in the execution and evaluation. If I delegate the organization of my lecture tours to an agency, it is because I cannot do everything myself. I invest my time where I am best. I don't want to lose days doing activities I don't like, not overcoming what is absolutely unnecessary. Where I feel the best—living in the wilderness—I am also the most effective. There is a market for the corresponding "byproducts," and the usual market laws apply. Over the course of years, I translated my success as a border-crosser more and more into financial success.

Financial Self-Sufficiency

Every expedition is also an investment. For the past 20 years, such trips have only been feasible when they pay for themselves. For 10 years, I have been involved in combining books and lectures, and as a consultant to manufacturers of sports equipment to increase the success of my mountain-climbing financially. A better strategy (through speed and easiness), has resulted in a better cost-benefit analysis every time. The 8,000-meter "hat trick" promised to be another step forward in this regard. While I understand that is an integral part of an expedition, I am developing self-understanding as an advertiser, but still according to the simplest solution. For 10 years, I have learned to minimize costs; now, the opportunity is offered to maximize benefits. I notice this already during the financing: publishers want the book and serial reporting in magazines about the series of climbs.

No Margin, No Mission

If I have been more impressive in the last 20 years than any other mountain-climber, this results not from the fact that I was better than all others. No, I have used myself much more strongly for my concepts. My pictures have been unique; they were understandable to everyone. The fact that this success could be exploited financially was just as important as the mountain climbing. But that is not what I live for. The concept of "border crossing" is filled for me with daydreams, curiosity, risk, and wildness. Money is involved only in the cost calculation. The revised values, however, correspond to a learning process—the real, most important profit, not money or moral or general well-being. In this connection there are no truths, only possibilities.

Financial Support

Any success I have enjoyed as a climber has come because I climbed with complete dedication. I planned to use this same dedication to finance my ideas and to be my own expedition leader. Early in my climbing career, there was no hope of balancing the books. When some money came in, then I could pay for the travel, equipment, or food. I did not then believe that an expedition had to be self-supporting. Today it is different: I only set out once an expedition is fully financed. Otherwise, it is impossible to climb for any length of time—unless you are very rich. It used to take me one or two years between expeditions to earn enough money for one of my special projects. So I became head of a climbing school, a lecturer, and an author. As long as I had a chance, however small, of recouping the money afterward, I felt good about setting off on a trip.

Return on Investment

If I am successful in a commercial sense today, it is because I am now reaping the "interest" from those early investments. It was a different matter in 1970, when hardly anyone thought I had the remotest hope of success with what I was doing. "Freelance mountaineer" was not exactly a recognized profession. Anyone who has the enthusiasm and willingness to put both their heart and soul into both the "fun" side and the "work" side will be successful. When it comes to realizing dreams, the most important prerequisite is the courage to think in a revolutionary manner. If I had an idea I wanted to develop, I would think it right through carefully, and only then seek support for it.

Financing Expeditions

Naturally I am also dependent on my sponsors. My idea must first be financed. I give my best also in this connection, although my time is limited, for I must train most of all. No helper can take training, preparation, and logistics away from me. No one else can develop the plan and implement it. It has become easy for me today to finance my expeditions. I am as proud of that as of my other achievements. I have not yet found a true sponsor, in the sense of someone who gives me money for my enterprises without hope of return, but I have made many contacts, and scoop in so many royalties from my books, that I can indulge my wildest schemes.

Climbing as a Profession

On 8,000ers it is not important whether you are a professional in the commercial sense, as I am, or an amateur. It is like art. A pro has no more time to train than an amateur, than someone who works in any other field of life. Whether you climb in your free time and are able to go on expeditions on your annual holidays, or whether you divide your time between mountain activities, lecture halls and management is unimportant. The only thing that matters is how seriously you take what you do, and how creative you can be at it. I finance not only my expeditions but also my life indirectly from climbing and directly from marketing the by-product of climbing. But I have to spend the greater part of my time in Europe writing books, standing on a platform, consulting with business partners, or designing improved items of equipment. It requires considerable professionalism to manage such a job successfully; and professionalism takes application, skill and time, which is then lost to training.

My Profession Is Life

People have no profession without experience. I know that our modern model society continuously prescribes a more compelling, specific type of education or cultivation. Doers in a minute line of human acts, not "opportunity workers," are given the job opportunities. I am also a specialist. Today we live in a gigantic performance machine. We are not able to do everything. But, some of us have opportunities to manage without a learned trade. I happily treasure such opportunities. I do not work in a profession, at least not in the professions I studied (surveyor, construction engineer, architect). Instead, I live. I do what I can do best. I also always alter my activities as an adventurer, as well as the evaluation of such activities. Strictly speaking, I am active in a half-dozen trades: as author, lecturer, photographer, miner, film maker, and guide for incentive groups. This densely populated world requires ever more specialization. Natural law is not the vocational scheme of people today. We Europeans are not as flexible and self-evident with changes of occupation as are the Americans, who change occupations about as often as they change their shirts. Income, success, extraordinary abilities, and ambition are thus of high importance in the USA.   MM

* * *

Application and Action:

Application: Knowing that no dream goes far without funding, how can you build better relationships with your sponsors, bankers, advisors and investors? How can you have them share in your success? What must you do to build and maintain credibility in the markets? Seek the best answers to these important business questions.

Action: Improve your "capital of credibility" and your financial proposals and presentations to facilitate the funding of your expeditions.   AA

Chapter 22
Strategy and Planning

With the end in mind and the means to fund the mission, you now face all the "how" questions surrounding strategy and planning. Messner generally prefers strategies that support the principles of "less is more" and "small is better" and "faster is safer" and "simple is the best structure" and "fair means is the right thing." In all this planning, however, Messner doesn't lock himself into a strategy that may not play well on the face under adverse conditions. He always gives himself the freedom to change and solve problems along the way—and the ultimate right and responsibility to turn back if absolutely necessary. The quest for success must not come at the expense of survival—human life matters too much to sacrifice people to reach a summit. So, in the end, Messner opts for an "on-site" strategy that allows for error and ensures survival.

✳　✳　✳

Doing the Right Things

My tours function like industry functions. Only without the hydrocephalus of excessive bureaucracy. In this, I was at first limited to a planning horizon that forced me to small, fast, "cheap" expeditions. I adapted my execution strategy to this. Planning is nothing more than anticipated decisions. For me, the primary thing is still, as before, doing the right things. Then, doing my things correctly. Being good at planning, execution, and evaluation corresponds to earnestness in the game.

To Plan or Not to Plan?

My strategy is to ascend so quickly that a "point of no return" is created. I will use events consciously to remain flexible during the execution. My 10 years of experience in the Himalayas contribute nothing to this project. Nevertheless, plans are only plans. Most of them cannot be maintained in the execution. In a border crossing, you can make as many plans as you want; they work seldom or never. The weather conditions and health circumstances cannot be calculated in advance. Still, it doesn't work without plans, either. Neither the top of Nanga Parbat nor the North Pole can be reached without definite logistics. But on-site improvisation remains just as important. The ability to play through everything in the plan and still remain open for all eventualities is part of the art in a game like mine to drive me to the top.

Solve Problems Along the Way

Staying balanced cannot be planned. I am balanced, and I know that uncertainties are hidden in action. So, I go forward! Once on the way, I try to solve all problems. "Do it, try it, fix it," say the business consultants of McKinsey. Climbing is like a contract with oneself. When a earthquake shook Nanga Parbat so strongly that thousands of tons of loose ice broke off and cut off my planned path, I went onward. It is like "fleeing forward." A voice says, "Somehow I will get out of this too." I gain a strong conviction to overcome everything. In my ascent to the top, I am very slow, because of bad snow conditions. I talk to myself repeatedly. Late in the afternoon, I reach the top. I have a strong desire to share my success with others, although I realize success can never given to anyone—never and nowhere.

Planning and Execution

Dreaming and planning are necessary but insufficient. It's like trying to make love in an empty room. Implementation is just as important—and just as difficult. To convert an idea into action, you need a positive attitude, hope, meaning. The consequence is usually joy in action. Many people have good ideas, but few have the ability to implement them. I experience this over and over again.

On my tours, minimizing equipment and costs have often been essential triggers of ideas. The idea was in planning and realization to facilitate what was primarily to be achieved through weight reduction. I have started some of my pioneering new mountain climbs as minimum calculations: With ever less aids, less weight, and ever less money, I improved my game possibility.

My ambition, my goals, and my circumstances in life forced me to this minimization calculation. As a South Tyrolean without a national background (Italian sponsors supported Italian expeditions, Germans supported German expeditions, etc.) I had to finance my ideas from a mini-market (South Tyrol). To advance to the realization of greater goals, I was forced either to cooperate with national expeditions or to realize my ideas by myself on a mini-budget. I decided on the second option very early.

Logistics and Strategy

Since the beginning of my mountain trips abroad, I realized that the old, classical form of Himalayan expeditions was outdated. But it took a long time before I knew how I could rise out of this system, which had been established for nearly a century. I looked for alternative strategies for a long time. Then I had to learn how to implement them seriously.

In the pyramid form of an expedition, many valley bearers (often 1,000), mountain-climbers, and high bearers work together under the strict leadership of an expedition leader to enable one, two, or three people to get to the top at the end. The logistics are similar to those of a small industrial operation. In the lower camps, many tents and supplies and equipment are needed. The less-trained bearers and mountain-climbers are used there. All those who supply the upper camps are there.

Proceeding upward, there are fewer who climb and drive the ascent forward.

This structure requires not only many materials—often 10 or 20 tons—but also a great deal of organization. Thus a large expedition lasts a long time. It is dangerous because of the frequent bad weather, which on the great mountains of the world can have overwhelming consequences (avalanches!), are dangerous, and also do not promise much success. Periods of beautiful weather cannot be exploited rapidly because of the difficulty of the equipment.

Simple Structure and Speed

I needed five years before I knew how the shape of my expeditions should look. In this five-year maturation process, I had a vision for the first time. I wanted simple structures and speed. That was possible only with more self-responsibility and fewer materials. A troop directed by an organizer did not come close to my ideal, but a team that functioned according to a democratic pattern. In the best case, I needed only one partner. In addition, I wanted to organize few steps in advance and to make many decisions spontaneously on the mountain.

This had been my style also in Alpine mountain-climbing. It corresponded to my essence. My goal was to start a practical attempt. To convert this utopia into action became dominating in my life. Certainly I had also been curious before. I had always kept a look-out for new paths and strived to expand my limits—in mountain-climbing and on my own—farther outward. Now a new style was evolving. I brought no computer with me for my first two-man expedition to an 8,000-meter peak, for working out logistics and strategies. I wrote the cost calculation on an envelope—also the individual steps for getting to the summit, including risks and chances for success. The real calculations would start when we started climbing the mountain.

Lightning-Fast Action

Thinking dogmatically and behaving in the usual way should be prevented in any enterprise. Why couldn't my new expedition style become faster, promise more success, and be less dangerous? There are few people in the game. We few could react faster to outbreaks of bad weather and get down the mountain faster, then climb up again faster than is possible with a large group.

The strategy of my smallest expedition looked different than that of a traditional large undertaking. I wanted to use periods of good weather without preparatory work, to get up the mountain as high as possible , then descend to return to the base camp as if fleeing. The important thing was not the preparation and not staying on the mountain, but lightning-fast action.

Two people make a democratic team. Natives will be used as bearers only as far as the base camp. They are thus no longer water bearers to the victor, as the Sherpas have been for decades. They have hauled loads through the most dangerous zones of the approach, just so that a couple of climbers could get to the top "on their backs."

Semi-Autonomous Work Groups

Breaking an expedition down in to the smallest possible units (valley bearers as far as the base camp, expedition kitchen there only, one or two rope groups on the mountain), whereby each unit assumes its own task, guarantees flexibility and effectiveness. Each of these groups controls itself with the greatest possible self-responsibility. Material flows are reduced to a minimum. In addition, decision processes are accelerated, and environmental damage is minimized.

Quality of Life

My kind of border crossing is damned by opponents as an "ideology of madness." In western society—oriented toward performance, money, and material profit—my statements seem like a contradiction: on the one hand, I refuse to modernize my means; on the other hand, I maximize my success. But refusing to go high tech has absolutely nothing to do with refusing to perform. I can accomplish more because I refuse technology and helpers. I could go to the North Pole on a "Skidoo" or in an airplane, there and back, but this doesn't appeal to me. In a border-crossing, I want to refuse airplanes and motor sleds from the start, not only to protect the environment but also to play the game by my own rules! If all of us were to park our cars this weekend voluntarily and start walking, if we were to refuse to turn on the television or use the telephone continually, we would become aware of values such as silence, harmony, and rest. Wouldn't that be a gain in quality of life?

Error-Tolerant Strategy

I include possible mistakes in the calculation. An "error-intolerant" strategy is inhuman. Maximizing profit cannot exist only in wanting to have more. We are using in one century on earth the energy that has been stored for millions of years. The profits from this are not used to develop new forms of energy; we use them up, forever. We have achieved a standard of life that is probably the highest that humanity has ever reached. Viewed purely economically, our system is working outstandingly. If, however, we do not learn to refuse certain luxuries voluntarily, we will be forced to refuse them.

On-Site Strategy

After my team-materials-weight calculation is ready, the starting date set, and the duration of the expedition outlined, I can think about an on-site strategy. But this depends on the weather, our acclimatization, and, not least, on our health. Thus, our procedures are open to a large extent. My efforts in working out the new strategy apply to the problem-solution relationship. Miniaturizing the expedition favors not only the elegance of the climb, but also cost expenditures. An expedition that moves 10 tons to the base camp—often preceded by long flights and approach paths, costs a great deal of time and money. If I can do the same thing with one-hundredth the weight, a large expedition can no longer be justified.

Everest Survival Strategy

We seem to have lost sight of the fact that humans cannot survive at heights approaching 9,000 meters. As more of us climb where we don't belong, the accidents will increase and, with them, so will the desire to make such an attempt. Treading the footsteps of those before them, waiting in line at the Hillary Step below the summit, more people climb to heights that offer no retreat for the inexperienced when storm, mist, or avalanche play havoc with fuddled brains.

What makes Mount Everest so dangerous is not the steepness of its flanks, nor the vast masses of rock and ice that can break away without warning. The most dangerous part of climbing Mount Everest is the reduced oxygen in the summit region, which dulls judgment, appreciation, and feeling anything at all. With modern, lightweight oxygen apparatus, the mountain can be outwitted. But what happens when the bottles are empty, when descent through a storm becomes impossible, when you can go no further? An Everest climb cannot be planned like a journey from Zurich to Berlin, and it doesn't end on the summit.

In any sports shop you can buy, for a price, the lightest equipment there is, but you cannot purchase a survival strategy. You surrender responsibility for yourself to the guide, and the higher the mountain, the more personal responsibility you willingly yield up, even though this is the basic prerequisite for any tough experience. And what happens when the leader gets into difficulty? You are left hanging in the ropes on a mountain you neither know nor understand.

Small Expeditions

One of the best mountain climbers, expedition leaders, and strategists of the last 25 years is Chris Bonington, a British man. He led a classic expedition in 1970 to the South Wall of

Annapurna and invented a new style. The new thing in this expedition was not only in the difficult goal—the South Wall of Annapurna, 3,500 meters (11,483 feet) high, one of the steepest Himalayan walls—but in a new set of facts. Bonington made decisions on the basis of factual logic, and threw many of the traditional ideas and ideals overboard. And he had success with this. In the same style, he organized and led the Southwest Wall expedition to Mount Everest in 1975. Next, he created the small expedition—out of the recognition that after crossing the most difficult wall on the highest mountain, the expedition style also had to be changed. Although today most expeditions to the highest mountains have gone back to the outmoded camp style—or else small expeditions have silently grown on the mountain into gigantic conglomerates—I believe that small expeditions that act faster and are easier to finance will be implemented once all national feelings and club interests have been satisfied.

Futuristic Visions

My strategic visions always have another breeding ground. This is how the small expedition arose, because it is more elegant, cheaper, and ecologically cleaner than a large expedition. It is future-related in every aspect, and it has therefore changed high mountain-climbing. Even a business enterprise acts ecologically when it thinks futuristically.   **MM**

* * *

Application and Action:

Application: In light of this management wisdom from Messner, reexamine your strategy for success and survival in your field. Does it give you the flexibility you need to adapt quickly and take advantage of changing market conditions? If not, revise it to reflect today's need for speed and flexibility.

Action: Devise and implement a "fast and flexible" strategy in your organization.   **AA**

Chapter 23
Companions and Teams

The myth and the metaphor of the harmonious "rope team for life" breaks down in the heat and cold of the climb, and in the harsh climate of the aftermath, with the inevitable tensions. But the fact remains that trust among companions boosts the odds of success and survival during the climb. So, while Messner derides the myth, he manifests the reality of functional relationships. He champions deep and meaningful involvement with team members, building relationships of trust, and sharing things in common without concerns about rank and command. He promotes and practices the ideal of "equal partners with equal say" and "groups with a common goal." Realizing that he can't achieve some goals alone, he seeks the right combination of companions and teams to put himself and others in a position to reach the top.

✳   ✳   ✳

Rope Groups

There are heroes only in the fantasies of those who want to be heroes. In marriage also, a critical observer might ask whether and to what extent this "rope group for life" corresponds to a wish or a suppression mechanism. A group that is bound by time and goals—a rope group—need not establish an ethical value of camaraderie. A rope group should be triggered at the right moment. One must be able to go separately. No one can be forced to stay together for a long time peacefully. I am suspicious of all the "selflessness" that leads others through deserts or moves mountains at work. Anyone who seeks to justify himself in his actions has a poor self-concept.

Pulling Together

I have made over 60 trips in the nature of an expedition. In this I have had minor difficulties with fewer than 200 people. Serious difficulties with my partners—whether a group with a purpose or a friendship—have never arisen during the border trips, even when the situation was stressful or hopeless. The ability to live and climb together is half of the success on any venture. We pulled ourselves together. Over and over again we compromised and found a common solution to the predicament we faced. If a break occurred between me and my partners, it was exclusively after the expeditions, after great successes. Anyone who hopes to rejoice in his accomplishments must not feed his feelings with anger, aggressiveness, jealousy, or revenge just to be able to gloat. The trick is to pull together.

Breaking Up

Some break-ups between me and my climbing companions occurred because my partners found it hard to be stars next to me. Some even made capital out of labeling me as a monster or falsifying the facts. I am glad to take part of the blame on myself, if I made it difficult for others to profile themselves next to me. In this, I should have taken into account the fact that I did not profile myself on the others. Not only have some climbers profited from me, they profiled themselves on my image. With an eye to their own profits and behind the protection of a false official ideology of camaraderie, they and some others tried to go "over my dead body."

I have defended myself without criticizing the corresponding group after the fact. Disappointments with families also led to the wish to do everything alone, to lead everything alone to the end, to create everything myself. And this wish has grown even stronger after my solo trips. In this, the need to be able to do "all" was not as much in the foreground as a strong need for autonomy and autarchy. The fact that with my solo trips I broke the last taboo of the Himalaya priests made me better known, but it did not contribute to making me loved in mountain-climbing circles. So in my private life I became more and more a solo traveler.

For too long, I complained about everything and thus wore myself out and all those who stood by me. In this, I made the error of seeing the reason for being in my partner for life. But I can work well in a rope group. I have found partners over and over again. Many rope groups have lasted for years, even decades. Others have broken up after a few undertakings.

Involvement With Each Other

A team functions outstandingly when life and death are involved. No rule of living together is violated then. People at risk typically live and work together correctly. So, in every new rope group, a deep involvement with each other must take place. In contrast to a partnership, which can be dissolved at any time without being bound from the beginning to a certain distance, I am bound unconditionally to my team during the border crossing. Some "deceptions" and "manipulations" may actually turn out to be helpful in getting along, and I sometimes utilize them to motivate people to peak performance. The most gifted people can deceive a deceiver. But usually members of a rope group are able to get along. Egotism is not directed against the others, but against the common goal.

Trustworthy and Friendly

Being friendly to each other is a basic requirement for success. During an undertaking, trust is also required in addition to ability and identification with the common goal. I am especially sensitive about this last point. If the trust relationship with a partner is disturbed, even in the least, I can do nothing more with him. To tell me and the others that a consensus could exist, is not my thing. A "broken" rope group, like a broken marriage, will not hold. You can perhaps deceive others for a short period of time, but you cannot deceive yourself.

Weak and Strong Members

Although I have always tried not to proceed according to the old expedition patterns, I have also had unpleasant experiences with people. Typically, everyone thinks about himself at first, and a team is only as good as its weakest member. The weakest one determines the tempo. In climbing the large mountains, there are fewer of these problems. We start at a base camp, climb up, and then come back to it. We approach the summit in a swinging motion. We acclimatize and prepare ourselves. In this phase, it becomes clear who are the strongest members of the team. And the strongest ones go together, normally, to the top at the end. One can also wait a thousand meters below the summit while the other ascends further and returns.

Share in the Rewards

On my first 8,000-meter expedition (Nanga Parbat), the contract prohibited me and my companions from creating reports on our own. We were all required to obey this contract. After the expedition, fees for approved lectures and books were to be paid to the leadership of the expedition. I have never forced such a contract on my partners, even when I financed the expedition. I believe in sharing the rewards of success.

Give Partners Your Trust

On the Antarctic crossing, we had to stay together. Nevertheless, I have no claim to uncritical loyalty beyond the expedition. But I do expect honesty. With partners who later deceive me or exploit me, I cannot plan any further undertakings. In exchange for identification with my project, I give the partners my trust. I expect theirs. If this relationship of trust is disturbed, there is also no rope group as a group with a purpose. In a small team, every individual is needed; no one can be left behind. And so you learn to resolve disputes by compromise. Whoever doesn't want to be left behind goes. You must build realities and explain them to the partners—even communicate them as collective realities.

Share Common Goals

The prejudice, which has been repeated thousands of times, that a group can only succeed when it consists of friends, is anchored so deeply that many are driven to failure with "mountain camaraderie." Naturally, a group of friends can also go far. When ability, experience, and will are distributed approximately equally in such a team, the chances of success are increased through the friendship. But even two or more individuals who are the best in their field can go far without being friends. I have mostly built my expeditions on common goals. Each rope group has been bound by time and goals, not conceived in advance as a "rope group for life." There are no border-crossers among my best friends that I could go to the end of the world with them. My friends are important to me because we have things in common.

During my years of climbing and expeditions, friendships were often formed during and after the travels together. But these friendships were not planned in advance. They were accidental. The camaraderie, which is so highly praised by Alpinists especially, was almost always there during the trip. If I sometimes resist using the word "camaraderie," it is because it is used too much, and many people give it false connotations.

Counterfeit Camaraderie

When there is talk of "camaraderie," "getting into one another," and "being interdependent," there is often hypocrisy. For example, one partner dedicated his book of remembrances to "the rope group" as if to set up a memorial to camaraderie in general, and he mentioned examples that helped him to this important recognition. First, the 1938 rope group on the north wall of the Eiger. Two Austrians were on the wall when two Germans came from behind and overtook them. As stated in the original reports, some words were exchanged. Only against their will and because of the bad weather conditions did the two rope groups combine. When they remained on the wall, it was because there was no other way. Only together, in a group of four, did they have a chance of coming off the "wall of death" alive. And the four mountain-climbers could do little when Hitler exploited the merger of the two rope groups as a symbol for the annexation of Austria. He idealized the rope group only to arouse emotions. But later, little was left of this rope group. The four men never again climbed together in a rope group; in fact, they hardly saw each other again. In other examples of the "rope group as an association for life," the same theme emerges. There can be no talk of friendship in connection with these groups. They were usually forced to travel together, because they could not survive alone. Later, nothing was left of most of these idealized rope groups.

Wall of Walls

In 1975 as a large team of Italian mountain climbers, we want to climb the "most difficult 8,000-meter wall: the south wall of Lhotse." On the left, flattest part of the wall, we only get to 7,800 meters. There are too many of us. Obviously, others are suffering from the same dualism as I: They like to belong to a group, but at the same time, everyone wants to be profiled as a star. I come to realize that smaller units with highly motivated fellow climbers are more successful than large teams.

In March 1989, one climbing generation later, I organize an expedition to the south wall of Lhotse myself. Again, this is a diverse group. Most are stars back home. I do not want to go to the peak. I see my role this time differently than in 1975. As a catalyst in the group, I will motivate the strongest rope group to get to the summit. There is a big difference between reaching the summit yourself and organizing an expedition for others. The stress is lower when you don't have the top as your goal. The summit goal puts a lot of pressure on your courage. It often makes a trip unpleasant. At first, this expedition seems to be more refreshing than all 29 of my 8,000-meter expeditions, in which I struggled to reach the top.

We gradually learn to know each other and get a feel for each other. Without a readiness to recognize your reflection in others, you won't have a strong team: Personal egotisms are concealed; justifications start; and helplessness spreads. Only when each individual organizes himself and sets himself up the way he likes can the base camp become comfortable. And without a peaceful base camp, staying under the wall becomes agony. It then costs too much energy.

How much easier it is to organize a regional or national expedition than an international one! Here, there are as many mentalities as participants. After discussing our governing principles, we make the decision to work together from the start. We adopt a tactic with two summit teams. We determine to prepare a route on the right wall and use this route for the ascent, escape, and acclimatization. At the end, everyone will be free to climb as high as he wants.

Some climb down to the base camp and state that they want to travel home. Their self-confidence seems to be poor. Everything else is excuse. I don't try to hold them back. Anyone who cannot identify himself with a project becomes a brake. The realization that as a catalyst I have no power if I don't want to get to the top myself comes too late. In all 50 of my previous mountain expeditions, I have reached the top if anyone did. If I didn't go to the highest point, no one else did either. But how freeing are expressions of irritation, rage, and self-doubt! We bring the equipment from the wall and end all attempts at the summit. I learned that a strong team does not arise with the vision of an individual. It is based on common consciousness. All must want the same thing. With a team you force into being, you won't get far.

Group with a Goal

I go wherever I want. For my goals, I look for partners who are most like me. I can be successful in a team only when my partners are enthusiastic for the common goal. We border crossers always work in small groups. Even two can be a rope group, a team. And my teams are defined by a common goal. I choose my partners accordingly, often from strangers. In mountain climbing, it was simple for me to form rope groups. I knew many good climbers. We fit together because we absolutely wanted to ascend the same wall. So we climbed together. Friendships and short-term groups with a purpose were formed out from this common bond. Friendship in a rope group is not necessarily a plus. I would rather go into a difficult situation with a stranger than with a friend. The older I become, the more my friends have disappeared from the ranks of possible climbing partners. Some have died; others have given up. Most mountain-climbing friends of my age have gone into a civilian profession. They are so busy with their tasks that they cannot come with me on my border-crossings. They don't have the time or the necessary energy.

Equal Partners

In 1986 I was a newcomer to ice hiking, and I didn't have a friend who was familiar with ice hiking. So I looked first in my own cultural circles for a partner with experience. I didn't want to communicate at the South Pole with foreigners in a foreign language. I contacted the most experienced man at that time in the German-speaking region. I came to him through a mutual friend—a process that has legal ramifications, since those making the invitations for a difficult expedition could be sued as instigators in case of an accident. There were other good men—Norwegians, Canadians, and Englishmen—who knew these types of border-crossings better than any German-speaking pole traveler, but a common language and a common goal were the two basic requirements in our partnership. Two or more people who want to be equal partners with the same vehemence form a strong team.

Two Is Not Too Many

I must accept that partners are the most important support in border crossings. Two is not too many. The minimum calculation as a game possibility is not enough. Reality stays hidden within itself, undetectable. Walking alone is just walking. Running ahead and behind begins with a crowd. In the group, decisions must be reached together. To remain flexible and react together in unforeseen conditions means a loss of time in the group and also often a penalty in terms of energy. The concept of "minimum calculation" means to assemble small, effective teams and let them grow through several difficult situations to a full unfolding of their effectiveness. My partners did not have to "keep quiet and function." They had to subject themselves not to me, but to tasks they set for themselves. The motive is determined by the spirit of a border-crosser. Planning models and management theories are side issues for this.

Equal Say

I do not control the input of my companions. Each of us has an equal say, and each is as responsible as I for the outcome of the expedition. I have not made my companions sign any form of contract before we started, binding them to absolute obedience or forbidding them to write anything about the expedition. My job, as I saw it, was to raise the bulk of the money for the expedition, provide the team with the best possible food and equipment, lead them to the mountain, and to be prepared on the most dangerous passages to climb out in front. Financing was only possible with press and television contracts, support from the trade, and help from private patrons. Naturally all that raises expectations, but I never raise false hopes.

I Can't Do It Alone

The practical side of my life has been shaped to an extent by my predecessors, in as much as I have learned many mountaineering ideas from history. I knew that the only way I could do something "new" was to know what everyone had done before. I have modeled myself on Walter Bonatti, Hermann Buhl, and Paul Preuss—even when it came to developing new techniques for negotiating lecture fees or advertising contracts. All three not only achieved exemplary work with their climbing deeds, they stood also as examples of how to organize a life as an independent adventurer. Apart from the few friends that I have, they have given me the most practical help. I could not have done it alone. Also, without the support of the readers of my books, the people who come to my lectures, and my fans, I would have starved emotionally, would have given up somewhere along the line. And, without the trust of my business partners, I would never have been in a position to get so far, and certainly not to the top.   **MM**

*   *   *

Application and Action:

Application: How strong are your rope groups and summit teams? What might you do to be a better team member or leader? How can your team or group achieve the unity in purpose that makes great accomplishments possible?

Action: Create teams as needed for certain climbs, expeditions, projects, and adventures and seek the kind of meaningful involvement with members that creates a common bond and ensures a shared reward.   **AA**

Chapter 24

Leading People

From the beginning to the end of the climb, the ability to lead people often makes the difference in outcomes. The proof of real leadership is in the success of the venture. Even if the summit is not reached, most goals are met. Messner often allows for leaders to emerge during an expedition, perhaps even to change roles under extreme circumstances. Leadership is not a contract, position, title, or appointment but rather the projection of a personality who has the courage to assume the challenge. In the Antarctic, Messner demonstrates the "emotional intelligence" that every great leader possesses in working with different people and personalities toward meeting a shared objective. Leaders are "action artists" who shake people out of sleep, radiate something special, speak for the group, and push for the summit. What is most needed today are more visionary and inspirational leaders.

* * *

Unbeatable Leadership

Anyone who as a leader creates a team around himself, in which everyone pursues the same goal with vehemence, becomes successful and virtually unbeatable. My leadership in this connection has often been criticized as "people eating" or planning the careers of partners who often collided with each other, leading to some breakdowns. Our joint successes, however, prove that the spirit, planning, and execution on these expeditions have been correct.

Border-Crossers in Action

Leadership is all about action. No robot "ticks" like a bor-der-crosser in action. You can move your mountains, if you discover, track, and express your own unique potential. Record your ideas and incorporate them to give motivation for action. Your mental energy grows with clear thought and positive feelings, just as physical strength and endurance grow with training. So, put your convictions to a test. Exchange experiences in discussions with specialists; test your ideas in small steps. Self-understanding wants to come out of you like a shout of joy—so risk the "primal scream" (but not in the office or a train station) and rejoice about the change that is taking place in you. Several similar "ticks" encourage you to solve "impossible problems." Thinking as a totality of concrete connections precedes action. Decision fol-lows recognition of right and wrong. Your own right and wrong requires the courage to say "yes" and "no." The more challenging the game, the less often it is won.

Leaders and Followers

Everyone, except for the solo traveler, is a part of a rope group, a team. A rope system, according to the anarchic view, has been superimposed on the leadership system according to the old pattern. False vision: a group stands behind the flag. True vision: two or more, each the best in his field, go far, even without friendship. Rope groups are mostly bound by time and goals. Camaraderie and friendship are accidents. A rope group has fluidity—it comes together, then separates again. In my rope groups, everyone is free, before and after, to do what he wants (write books, give lectures, do advertis-ing, etc.) Dissolve the rope group at the right moment. Requirements for a strong rope group include: trust, ability, same goal, identification with the project. The repeated insight of having been disappointed undermines the strongest will. I don't like to give orders. I expect that the per-son I am arguing with can obey to his own will.

Leading Personalities

I do not hold with the old leadership patterns in which an expedition leader—with "no matter what" justification—gives orders, and the others have to obey. Nevertheless, I am convinced, there is always one "lone wolf." He takes from the others not only information, but also energy.

The leading personality has, on the whole, more experience, more endurance, and more charisma than all the others. Therefore, the others obviously give him the leadership. It happens silently. How the leading personality is selected is determined by rites. This group behavior is archaic. If someone attempts to take the leadership without being proven to be a leader, without appropriate qualifications, he will not be recognized as a leader. I have experienced times in which roles have changed, through an accident, shock, or illness—in seconds. The one who had set the tone, taking strength from all others, was suddenly no longer the leader. Someone else made decisions. The "strong man" from before suddenly had to give energy to the leading personality. It's a dangerous moment for the leader who has to give back or give up.

Courage to Lead

Courage to be egotistical is a requirement for a balanced life—especially for a leader. In my expeditions, I was usually a leader from the beginning. First, because I only go on expeditions that make me grow. Then, I decide on the goal and the method before I look for partners. I thus plan things alone, up to a certain point. When I notice something, I would like to do it that way. I provide myself with as many partners as together we feel necessary. It may be that the first partner talks me out of any others. From the time we commit to each other, we are a democratic team. No leader takes over, is elected, or prescribed. He becomes and remains such only thanks to a clear superiority.

Free from Contracts

In 1970, during my first 8,000-meter expedition, I was a member. As an invited participant, I had to pay my share and sign a contract. The expedition leader—he was also the organizer who had certain rights and obligations established in this contract—was weak in leadership on the mountain. We planned the ascent to the top on our own initiative. After that, we participants were forbidden from any kind of "muzzle contract," setting up an independent court.

Since this experience, I have always avoided expedition contracts. I have never concluded a contract with one of my partners. Everyone in my team could and can do what he wants. Also, everyone is free, before and after, to sell what he wants. On the way, we talk everything through together.

Leader on Paper

Who the leader is on paper remains a secondary issue. Many expeditions (in Pakistan, Greenland, and Nepal) must be approved, and an expedition leader must be stated each time. When I enter my name on the corresponding line under "leader," this is far from meaning that I will also hold the position of expedition leadership on the way. I respect the laws of nature, and even at the top, I have never had the feeling that I am stronger than the mountain. The earth is less undiscovered than human beings. All paths that have not yet been taken, all games that have not yet been played, are also potential possibilities for insight into our potential.

Doing It Alone—Together

Being able to "do it yourself" completely and still be together is possible in mountain climbing in a group. In the winter of 1992 in Greenland, for example, I wanted to see how it is when three people—two with the same language and one with a second language—go together, whether this silent change of leadership still functions. It does. It must also be this way in the world of work. In small groups, such as in parts of a company, there is always a dominant leading personality. He may not give orders, but he leads. His word carries weight.

Leading to a Common Goal

We hesitate to use the word "leader." As border-crossers, we need to pay attention to the language we are speaking. There enough "victories," "attacks," and "blitzkriegs" in the mountain books. We adventurers must get away from the language of war: Summits are not "conquered," walls are not "attacked," ice fields are not "possessed." We are also not pursuing any kind of political or ethical values. We realize an idea, at most. And the group does not stand "behind the flag," but before a common goal. In human consciousness, there are many truths, realities, and worlds, side by side.

Tale of Two Leaders

October 1989—Since ice hiking is strange to mountain-climbers, I look for personalities with strong will and conviction from other fields of adventure. The German seaman Arved Fuchs, a navigator with Arctic experience, can identify with my plan, after some initial skepticism. The question of who will lead us does not arise, after we decide to start as equal partners. Before setting out, we both know that we must go about 30 kilometers per day to reach McMurdo by February 15, 1990, that the longest stage to be traveled without intermediate depots (South Pole to McMurdo) is 1,500 kilometers (930 miles) and will be difficult (mountains and glaciers with crevasses).

After three weeks, I know that at our current rate the crossing of Antarctica cannot be accomplished. Arved resigns. He says he will be satisfied with reaching the South Pole. "Only the Pole counts with people," he says. For myself, however, the crossing counts. So I have to bring Arved, silently, to think the same. In this, he must not lose self-respect and must also improve in his conditioning. I can't do the latter. To train him, to go a quarter of an hour longer than agreed, would only bring a few additional kilometers per day and mistrust.

My recommendation—to repack the sleds in such a way that we could make the same speeds with different sled weights—eliminated the skepticism at first. I communicate the meaning of my tactic by emphasizing the positive for Arved: "This way, we can go faster and will reach the South Pole before New Year. This means for you that you will then be the first person to reach the North and South Poles within a single year." A record!

Only this ability to place himself in the foreground— which Arved Fuchs first ridiculed as record-seeking— inspired him. This record was only available to him, not me. Since I can still go as fast as before in spite of the heavier sled and am setting the tempo as the lead man, we are now making in the seven hours that Arved has used before for my six hours, up to 28 kilometers per day. He is still going behind me, but he does so willingly. Day after day I support his ability to be proud—proud of the second pole beckoning within one year, proud of the endurance to withstand the strain of Antarctica after more than 50 days of toil at the North Pole. This pride works wonders. The tricks I am using to motivate Arved serve my goal of a joint crossing. I know that success depends on both of us. Neither should remain behind. One would not get far alone.

On December 31, 1989, New Year's Eve, we reach the South Pole. With a flask of red wine, I arrange a small celebration for Arved and his record: two poles within one year.

The hope of being able to use a sail from the South Pole to the Ross Sea with a tail-wind, inspires Arved to go on. I am now confident. But our hopes are dashed. Because of the heavy sleds, light snow, and great difficulties (crevasses, broken ice), our speed drops again below an average of 20 kilometers per day. Because of the approaching winter and the departure of the "Barque," the ship for voyage home, in Baja

Terra Nova (Italian research station north of McMurdo) on February 15th, we are in a hopeless situation.

Arved pleads to make the sleds lighter and to break off the crossing at Gateway. I myself am considering giving up. I also refer to the costs and difficulties that would be involved in flying out from Gateway. I hope for a miracle and keep driving my partner onward. When a more favorable wind comes again, we make good ground, but not as much as necessary, because Arved's endurance is not sufficient for using a sail as long as the wind lasts. I am doubtful. But I restrain the rage, which sometimes boils high in me when Arved lags behind by kilometers, inside me or let it roar out into the white, cold ice world if he is so far behind me that he can't hear me. In turn, Arved also spared me from his outbursts. So he remained receptive to my subtle manipulations. But the snow is still cold. In the Antarctic, a tactic like that of the Himalayas (anyone who can't keep up stays back in the base camp) doesn't work. We have to continue to get along without fighting and make compromises.

At the end of January, at Gateway, Arved pleads once more to break off the expedition. I reach for my last trump card. He will get the tent, the Argos equipment (a satellite-supported positioning device that reports our position to the outside), and wait until someone comes for him. "I'll pay for this flight, but I will go to McMurdo!" I know that making this statement will lead either to the end of the expedition or else force him to bring forward the last ounce of self-motivation. I am lucky and win. Arved will go on.

In early February 1990, in spite of new snow, "white-out," and hunger (we had rationed the food, as a precaution), we go to the limits of performance. Often more than 30 kilometers a day, which I not only expect of Arved, but have confidence that he can do it. He now turns out be willing and able to perform. At this point, I explain to him again what it would mean—including financially—to arrive too late. Although I have financed the expedition myself, this information helps to increase my partner's motivation. I also state that one of the sponsors could pay for the a rescue flight to New Zealand for both of us, whose lives would be in danger if we arrived too late. (I later paid for it myself out my own pocket.)

But the most important thing was still that I went in front. The tent was in my sled, Arved had to come afterwards. In this, I understand myself only as a driver, not as an expedition leader. I wanted no firm rank, and I know that a prejudice for hierarchies is usually inversely proportional to real personality values. Although Arved and I are two completely different characters and come from opposite parts of nature sports (mountain-climbing and sea travel), we supplemented each other in the crossing of Antarctica ideally. We did not fit together, but our different capabilities added to each other. I was not driven in this by a will to perform, but was driven by a pressure to perform (a lot of money was at risk, responsibility with respect to the sponsors, widespread public expectation).

The best entertainment, and at the same time the strongest incentive, has something to do with dedication. We arrived on February 13, 1990; through a miracle, favorable wind had accelerated our progress during the last days. Our original tactic did not work, and so we found a new one, day after day for 90 days. I came to know Arved, and he came to know me.

Doing the Impossible

In the Antarctic, I first tried to communicate joy to my partner by psychological tricks. I was able to take some sled weight and some work away from him to make his life easier. In the second half of the trip, my tricks became rougher. This involved making 800 kilometers (500 miles) in 20 days. That was a "sheer impossibility," but it worked. Arved said over and over again, "I won't do that; I can't do that; I'll be killed; I'm not crazy!" But with the tent in my sled, I was able to force him to come along. In the first week after Gateway, I waited during the rest periods. By noon, Arved had then negotiated the nine hours of traveling to be done down to eight. I braked myself, and we limped through our quota. At the end, I became a rough taskmaster. I always went in front so that I saw Arved during the rest periods. When he got close, I went farther, until evening. He often came to the tent dead-tired, but he came. I found my methods terrible, and I asked myself: "Why am I torturing a person in this way? Is it just my ambition to get through?"

The Puzzle of Leadership

To lead an expedition to the end of the world, I need various capabilities. I must finance the undertaking, assemble and lead a team, and find and test equipment. Climbing ability, endurance, and training are obviously part of this as well. The most difficult thing is still putting ideas into action, withstanding critical moments. The evaluation (book, lectures, documentary film) is possibly part of the "aftereffects." All these various activities are a requirement for success in my field.

Gaining Global Perspective

In recent years, I have repeatedly started actions that require more than a usual border crossing. In my "March around the South Tyrol," the mountain-climbing side remained in the background. I was interested in a glimpse behind the scenes of the land. I saw my action primarily as a catalytic intervention, as a counterweight to the massive influence of politics and media on people. Border crossing approaches our need for self-clarity, inner freedom, meaningfulness, and uniqueness. My global perspective from the outside and the edge to the inside is a suitable balance to the narrow viewpoint of most politicians and media representatives, which is oriented toward the election cycle. While I believe in the creative power of spontaneous processes, I hoped by gaining "comprehensive" background knowledge to make a contribution to a self-understanding that cannot be obtained from advertising brochures, governments, or articles on the "threat to minority populations." Inspired by many personal exchanges of thoughts, being daily confronted with traffic problems, environmental disturbances, and Alpine economics, I wanted to give an impulse for something other than the usual way of looking at things. I needed a great deal of specialist and generalist knowledge, which I had to acquire first. I am neither a historian nor a politician or an ecologist. I am a person who is knowledgeable about politics, interested in history, and startled by ecology, who wants to be involved mainly in the land in which he grew up, lives, and wants to continue to live. I want most of all to exist for myself, only then for others

Leaders Shake People Out of Sleep

My path is not that of party politicians. I do not want to enter Parliament or the city council. So I don't need to seek for votes at election time. I say what I think, how I think it, mostly without embellishment. I only want to shake people out their sleep. I have never tried to be a folk hero, and I am used to rejection, especially at home. But, it it is not easy to proceed against so much misunderstanding. Still, I never tried very hard to curry favor with the critics.

Judged to be Illogical

Because I was still active as a mountain-climber, my South Tyrol action corresponded to both by ability as a hiker and climber and also to my intentions. My partner, Hans Kammerlander, is a self-confident South Tyrolean and a mountain-climber, like me. He's one of the best of the younger generation. A free-thinking partner, a series of discussions, the long march over the border mountains—this was the game plan. I did not expect that we would be judged afterward for what we tried to do for this land. If you still live outside of society, outside your opinions, outside your customs, outside your meaning, your code of behavior becomes illogical to other people around you. How often have I been almost in doubt about being a South Tyrolean!

Fitting Puzzle Pieces

Nothing has helped me so much toward so many recognitions as landscapes and their responses in my soul. Although I was the one who held all the reins in my hand, I concentrated completely on the sections of the path, individual discussions, and individual people. I had been referred to half a hundred helpers, contributors, and logisticians, and I still dedicated myself each time to the one who was with me at the time. As a "general entrepreneur," I was the system integrator and the responsible person. The expedition arose in this way first as a puzzle in my head, then on paper. People are naturally blessed with abilities, capabilities, and joys in life. Only when the puzzle pieces fit together do I have an overview.

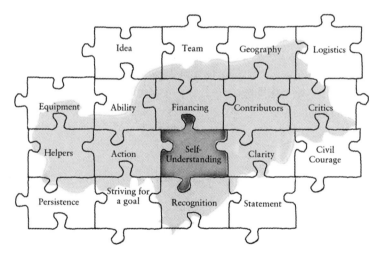

For this border march, important and unimportant things had to be coordinated equally. In the end, however, it was always my responsibility if something did not work out: if the photographer went to the wrong hut, the backpack came without climbing irons, or the film team arrived without cartridges. But since we basically had not forgotten anything, the march became a successful joint action.

Self-Expectations

Personal freedom grows less by what I expect from others than by what I expect from myself. Everyone must be able to express himself in his own way. I was certainly able also to make my know-how about mountain climbing available to younger mountain-climbers, and they were able to go around the land faster. In theory, the action could have been delegated. But it is not suitable for me just to propose an action, just to be a carrier of know-how. In almost all my actions, I have been an idea creator, strategist, and actor equally. In the end, I am also my own arbitrator. Border-crossings, as they become more difficult, can hardly be judged by outsiders.

Converting Ideas into Actions

Like adventures, actions also start in the head. However, the action pursues other goals than the border-crossing. It follows other criteria: it is not only a purpose in itself; it has more layers, more discussion partners, more coordination. Only when the entire puzzle can be viewed can I start to put the parts together. A good idea is so important, but realization remains the most difficult. As with border-crossers, the conversion of ideas into action is also the real art for action

artists. And only doing this leads to self-understanding. If I had stayed home in my office during the "March around the South Tyrol," I would have found no resonance and in the end nothing to say. Except for myself, I can see everything clearly when I'm in action.

My strong self-understanding could be transmitted onward also because ideas and actions had become one unit in my person. Thinking and negotiating were many times the same thing. When I walked, I talked. When I spoke, I thought. I did not ask myself then about the meaning of the undertaking, even less about whether it would be understood correctly by others. I could not transfer my self-understanding to others. But because I implemented the action myself and many questions had arisen in putting one stone on top of another, I have been inspired to consider the land as a whole. And this is what I had postulated as the actual goal of the undertaking.

Action Artists

Unfortunately, few border crossers (mountain-climbers, for example) have developed into "action artists." You might think that anyone who has learned to climb, cross ice, or survive in the wilderness for half a lifetime must in some way have become an action artist. Unfortunately, this is not so. One exception is Leo Dickinson, an excellent mountain-climber, wild-water runner, parachute jumper, and balloonist. He produced a documentary film during my Mount Everest expedition in 1978. Leo understood brilliantly his abilities and experiences and his enthusiasm for the wilderness, and he has converted them into films and books on the relationship of man-desert, man-mountain, man-ice, man-water, and man-air. "Filming the impossible" is the resumé of the man, who not only wants to climb as high as possible, travel as far as possible, and descend as deep as possible, but also has a need to present in words and pictures what is going on at the end of the world in the faces of the people. He has flown over the top of Mount Everest in a balloon, an action that has been attempted often and always failed. He achieved the balloon trip because he brought with him all the requirements and coordinated them all correctly and congenially.

Why I Hate Hierarchies

I hate hierarchies because I know that fixed positions are often inversely proportional to ability. I strive for democratic expedition leadership. Nevertheless, there is always one lead wolf: his supremacy, his presence, and his superiority give him more influence. A leader is a leader—both in small groups and in businesses A leader makes events, and events make a leader. A leader makes use of space and people, has charisma, energy, self-awareness, sensitivity, and readiness for responsibility. A leader creates self-understanding and evaluates his people; he uses their strengths and weaknesses; he keeps track of who is growing when and how. Charismatic creators of meaning —real leaders—are lacking in power politics.

One Speaks for All

In October 1992, I agreed out of curiosity to "lead" a group through the Takla Makan desert (Sinkiang). To act as a trip leader for the first time in 20 years was strange for me. Participants came together as individual tourists. There were 14 men, a mixed group who hardly knew each other. In contrast to border-crossing, where a good idea and good people are half the success, in my group a coupling is needed between individualism (self-consideration) and collectivism (all together) as the underlying culture. In a more difficult expedition, a motivating leading personality is in a position to spur average participants to above-average performance. On our desert trip, leadership involves communicating sensibly, without force, the belief that we will get through, and having confidence in all participants. On all my expeditions, asceticism in the exercise of power came in the middle. Often I simply started out. If I am not a useful leader, it is because some people have to torment others in addition to myself to remain stars. My ability to recognize performance is limited. I criticize too much and praise too little.

When we arrive, we learn that "our program" has been changed, over our heads. The group gives me the role of spokesman in negotiations with the local Chinese organizers. I accept the obligation "to push the cart forward." I argue half the night with the local organizers and elicit a vague promise that we can make a serious attempt to cross the desert.

When we start out on October 1, 1992, the local organizer is still threatening to force us into a camel tour around the Takla Makan. He states strictly that a crossing is impossible, probably because he received too little money from the travel organizer above him in Beijing. The Chinese require an extra charge. Everyone is agreed. The group stands unanimously together. This is already half of the success. We agree on a first compromise: the trip will be made from south to north. Negotiating with Chinese people and not "jumping over the table" is difficult. But when the group reacts so promptly, thinks together, and stands together, we are stronger than our counterparts. And this is true, even though we are a group that has been thrown together.

The group knows how and where the organizers can deceive us. So we discuss strategies to force the Chinese to do what they have promised. We all want to cross the desert together; the group is a team. Everyone agrees that punctuality is a positive discipline too. This positive way of living together functions without rules. Nevertheless, every participant has the greatest possible independence. We decide to stay with the camels. The danger of losing a member of the group is too great if everyone goes through the desert for himself. The combination of intensive action and extensive daydreams makes one creative.

The caravan is organized hierarchically. The caravan leader, Machmed, an old, thin man, decides everything. The men and animals belong to him. This hierarchy is so obvious that no one questions it—not his helpers, not the camels, not even we tourists. Machmed knows when the camels need water and how far the supplies will last. His orders must be obeyed by all. For decades, no one has doubted this. And his charisma grows with each march through the desert.

In the middle of the desert, the participants take turns going ahead with the compass and determining the route. In this way, everyone learns to navigate, gains self-confidence, and acts innovatively. The one leading decides how to get around the dunes. In the meantime, I am sure that we have developed so much self-confidence (positive culture) that the group can also withstand critical situations. It has no leader, and needs no leader. The culture is sufficient for us to proceed. I am only the spokesman. Everyone is making experiments and undertaking leadership tasks. No one is over-stressed. If the undertaking lasts even longer than expected, we could go a couple of days longer. The feeling of belonging grows with the resistance, and tasks are undertaken voluntarily. A team always has leadership; at least silent leadership. Leadership is assumed by the physically and mentally strongest personality.

Summit Leadership

When an Italian expedition started out for K2 in 1954, there had already been much dispute. This was not the first attempt at the second-highest mountain in the world. Three American expeditions with two excellent leaders, Fritz Weissner and Charles Houston, had failed. Ardito Desio, the leader of the 1954 expedition, was not an extreme mountain climber. He was a scientist, but he was convinced that K2 could be climbed. He had led the enterprise from below, with "a strong hand," according to all reports. His spirit and style were critical factors. Ardito Desio was capable, but he brought the expedition to a successful conclusion not because he led it authoritatively, but because he was accessible to ideas from the members of the group. He found the right balance between directing, stimulating, and self-responsibility of the participants. At the right moment, he assigned leadership of the summit team to a co-leader, Achille Compagnoni, who reached the top together with Lino Lacedelli.

Teamwork and leadership play important roles in mountain-climbing. I am convinced that on this 1954 K2 expedition, no Italian expedition leader other than Ardito Desio could have led the group, with its mixed nationalities and strong individuality, to the summit. He was the leader. During the expedition, no one doubted that. The fact that later everyone was eager to get to the summit and called himself the father of the success did not disturb Desio. He had contributed to the success. And that had been his only task.

Leaders Radiate Something Special

A leader can be questioned by his men and women during the undertaking; afterwards only if it has failed. Success gives him the right. I have always defined a team as a group of people who each wants the same thing with the same vehemence, even if only one of them has thought it up. This one is normally the leader. To achieve leadership strength, leaders also must collect ideas, maintain an overview, and take stands over and over again. Only in this way do charisma, self-understanding, and a leading personality arise. Contentment does not follow from satisfying all wishes. Leaders radiate something special because they *are* something special—not because they may have a special title or they have accumulated a special amount of power, knowledge, or money. The creative power of the leader is the more impressive the more "internalized" it is. As unnatural as this is, leadership involves holding to the self-chosen obligation in spite of things.

Democratic Leadership

The modern chief is a democratic leader. He does not create the rules and hierarchies in his team, but a climate of inspiration. He can listen from the inside and speak for all to the outside. Leadership can leap from one person to another. The leader takes energy from the others. Also because he does this more easily than the others. Even on small expeditions—which in my case are led democratically, meaning one man, one vote—there is one whose word counts for more. This person is often not the fastest or the strongest in the group. Maybe the initial idea didn't even come from him. But he does the leading. He becomes the leader through his presence, by showing the way, through quiet consideration.

How the Leader Becomes the Leader

How does a leader become clear in an expedition group? Mostly it happens little by little. In special, critical situations, in so-called "events." Events make leaders, and leaders make events. One of the group repeatedly comes forward in difficult situations. He takes the largest backpack, makes the decision, and assumes more responsibility. He is recognized by the others as the leader and has the ability to carry them away. By a series of successes of this kind and by his increased feeling of self-worth, the leader takes possession of people and the space in which they act more and more. Charisma grows further with each success, by the recognition of others.

Leadership Requirements

The requirements for being a leader are: first, a predisposition, then the opportunity to demonstrate it. A head start in experience, strength, and a feeling of self-worth are conceded to him. Anyone who doubts his action or has to have his leadership written up in a contract to force others to cooperate cannot be a leader for long. Also anyone who fakes superiority to bring recognition from others. A leader does not lead with arrogance or a tight hierarchy; he has good insights and gets involved in ideas and suggestions for improvement from his partners. I attribute many of my successes to a spontaneous idea of a partner. In 1984, Hans Kammerlander, in an attempt to reach both 8,000-meter peaks of Gasherbrum, made the recommendation to reverse my plan to climb from G I to G II, because the danger of avalanche in climbing G I turned out to be too great. This simple recognition assured the success.

Effective Style

Cooperation in the team is primarily important in the field of ideas. It is not the one with the hardest elbows that gets farthest, not even the diligent head-shaker or the "safety-over-risk official," but the daring daydreamer, the open idea-man who knows his way around less in numerical categories than in mental requirements, shares responsibility willingly, and thus multiplies the total creativity of his team. The "first man on the rope" is today nothing more than one who has more strength or more skills. Many people climb very well. For the first man on the rope, creativity is more important than technical knowledge. In addition, a combination of gifts, flexibility, and a style of his own are needed, along with a great deal of responsibility.

Leaders Climb in Front

The person climbing ahead is also thinking ahead. I don't want to claim to be a leader. It doesn't suit me to direct groups or lead with my know-how. But if I am going along myself, I get others to come too. I have been able to climb all 14 of the 8,000-meter peaks alone and have made 30 expeditions. I have failed 12 times. I have reached the top 18 times. And whenever anyone reached the top on these 30 expeditions, I was there too. I was thus able to lead my partners before the climb, during the climb, and during the action.

Sensitivity to People

A small group of people being on the way is also always an experiment, since we are always testing who is faster or weaker, who has how much self-understanding, who follows, and who leads. No matter how contradictory it seems, primarily in connection with myself, a leader shows more sensitivity than the others. Therefore, he knows how to evaluate the weaknesses and strengths of his partners and to use the whole group accordingly. In critical situations, he stands as a stationary pole in a group and helps it to master the critical situations. He applies encouragement and direction to his partners individually and in relation to the situation. In this, he does use the weaknesses and doubts of his fellow climbers in order to claim his leadership. He uses his consideration and his abilities and strengths to bear on all. Above all, the leader creates self-understanding. As he looks over his people, gets involved with them, and takes them along to a common goal, he can become a creator of meaning. Even more, he represents the ethics of their convictions, which everyone in the team is glad to follow, which each in turn receives as his own. The resulting group self-understanding, which lasts at least until the goal is achieved, permits everyone to grow—ideally, even to grow beyond himself.

Leader's Responsibility to Family

The leader also has great responsibility in the family dimension. The ethical question here is how much can a leader who is a spouse and parent risk and still act responsibly to family? As a father of children, I have to wonder whether I can be responsible for going on as a border-crosser: Could I be responsible for not doing what I do? Who could my closest relatives then rely on? I would no longer be myself if I couldn't lead my life. I would also no longer be this father for my children.

The fact that I have a family does not force me to change my life completely, to turn back so far that I give up my personality. Also, as the father in a family, I have the right to live my life. Through my children, I have become stronger, mentally speaking. For I can take them along on trips, at least in thought. For example, I had them along in spirit in Greenland. I take them in one of my spiritual levels from the end of the dream to the stage for the day. And they give me energy. In critical moments, they are an essential support for me to do everything right, to go on, to stand up again, and to come home.

During an expedition, I can occupy myself with the children; the children can do this less with me. That is unfair. Doubt and fears in connection with problems do good things, since through them energy fields develop in us that let us grow beyond our usual abilities. My wives have come to know me as an adventurer, as a possessed border-crosser. Their fears at home about me are probably not greater than in the family of a business manager.

Wanted: Visionary Leadership

The "normal citizen" can also learn something else from mountain climbers about restraint. Voluntary self-restraint is an order of the day. What the creators of religions have created can obviously not be done by the state. Visionary leaders are lacking. We do not need new religions and sects; we need strong personalities who can spread life attitudes related to our time, because they embody them and live them in an exemplary manner. To allow humanity to live a little longer in peace and relative "health" is a challenge to all of us. In this connection, visionary leaders are needed, worldwide. It is too late for defensive thinking. Now bold innovation and creativity are needed, not just finding the weaknesses in the ideas of others.

Inspirational Leadership

Away with all fixed hierarchies! On an expedition, the leader does not live in a larger tent. The head of a group of companies does not have his office on the top floor. He is one out of many. But his voice has more effect. The one to whom leadership is given and who is ready to accept leadership assumes responsibility for his own house. He speaks for the others as the representative of a group and as part of the whole. In every case, he embodies the culture of the group or organization and is a cornerstone in the conglomerate I call "the world ethic." If it should be necessary to go to another culture at the end of power politics—where powerful people are placed at the top ("chosen by God," and given the money, and the blessing of a large party), the leader of tomorrow must be capable of inspiring other people against the usual customs. **MM**

* * *

Application and Action:

Application: Assess your leadership of self, family, team and organization in light of Messner's lessons on leadership. How might you improve your leadership? Is your leadership visionary and inspirational? Do you know where you want to go— and are other people willing to follow your lead?

Action: Select three lessons on leadership from this chapter, put them in action in your life, and measure the difference your leadership makes over time. **AA**

Postscript

Surviving Success

by Sabine Stehle, participant in three 8,000ers

A life at Reinhold's side has absolutely nothing to do with the *dolce vita*, as many people (especially women) seem to think. In fact, it is quite the reverse. Travel is our freedom, but we have to pay dearly for it.

I know Reinhold needs publicity to achieve his style of life; and indirectly, he needs it emotionally as a confirmation of his total commitment to success. Celebrity or fame is something that everyone wants or thinks about at one time or another. And yet, the reality is very different from the dream.

With fame, you gain many advantages, especially material ones, but you have to give up so much for them, like your personal freedom. It becomes difficult to do anything spontaneous together, or to find privacy when everyone knows you.

Emotionally, Reinhold's life is like alternating hot and cold baths: hot when he is being showered with compliments and good wishes and everyone wants to know him; cold when he has to endure the spiteful attacks of critics. To be obliged to keep justifying yourself over things that are accepted in other people is not only wearing, but over time is discriminatory.

I have learned some important lessons from this: being famous is not all roses—it is a very hard condition, a difficult burden. Reinhold communicates to people an aspect of life to which they themselves have no entry. For that he receives

243

instant recognition and, indirectly, money. That means being careful. Without inner reserves and a sense of his own worth, he could very easily be consumed. Nobody makes a concession to a VIP, but everyone wants what he can get out of him.

As his fame spreads, as the number of admirers grows, so also grows the number of critics and "friends" who very quickly are no friends at all. Who would not become careful and mistrustful in such circumstances?

It seems to me to balance out like this: you trade in your freedom in your early life against pressures later; and earlier restrictions against current opportunities, according to how you look at it. The danger that Reinhold could have lost his personality under the pressure of publicity was great. But, to his credit, he has come through it, as he has through avalanches and storms. **MM**

About the Author

The world's most famous mountaineer, Reinhold Messner, was born in South Tyrol, Italy on September 17, 1944. He grew up in the Villnöss Valley in the Dolomites and began climbing when he was only five years old.

By the time he was 20, he had already made about 500 climbs in the eastern Alps. He introduced lightweight "alpine style" climbing to the world when he and Peter Habeler made a remarkable ascent of Gasherbrum I, without the use of bottled oxygen or fixed lines, and hardly any of the other equipment deemed "essential" by the climbers of the time.

He made history again in 1978 when he and Habeler accomplished the impossible, climbing Everest without oxygen. In that same year he pioneered a new route and climbed Nanga Parbat alone. Two years later, he succeeded in a solo expedition to the summit of Everest during the monsoon season, regarded as the greatest mountaineering feat of all time, and established his place as one of the world's greatest mountaineers.

Messner then set his sights on being the first to climb all 14 of the world's 8,000-meter peaks, which he accomplished on October 16, 1986, when he reached the summit of Lhotse. During that period he also became the first to score a "hat trick" by climbing three 8,000-meter peaks in one season.

After achieving that goal, he went on to set and achieve others, including climbing the tallest mountain on all seven continents. The last mountain he climbed to reach this goal was Mt. Vinson in Antarctica at a temperature of minus 50 degrees celsius. In 1990 he set another first when he was the first man to cross the Antarctic continent on foot.

When not off on an adventure, Messner lives in Juval Castle in South Tyrol where he runs an art museum and an organic farm. He also pursues his other careers as a writer, photographer, and member of the European Parliament. Messner also lectures throughout the world, makes documentary films, contributes articles to several magazines, and is an active preservationist of wilderness areas. He is the author of more than 40 books, which have been translated into a dozen languages, including *The Crystal Horizon, Everest: Expedition to the Ultimate,* and *All Fourteen 8,000ers.*

OTHER BOOKS BY REINHOLD MESSNER

All 14 Eight-Thousanders
When Reinhold Messner reached the summit of Lhotse in Nepal, he became the first man to stand on all 14 of the world's 8,000-meter peaks. This revealing memoir gives readers a glimpse of the preparation, organization, and running of Messner's expeditions, as well as rare moments on the summits of the world's highest peaks.

Hardcover book   **$40.00**

The Crystal Horizon
On August 20, 1980, Reinhold Messner, the world-renowned master of alpine-style climbing, became the first person to reach the summit of Everest solo and without supplemental oxygen. A vivid account of Messner's expedition, *The Crystal Horizon* also reflects on how he explored his innermost thoughts while facing the most extreme physical challenge he had ever encountered.

Paperback book   **$24.95**

Everest: Expedition to the Ultimate
In this mountaineering classic, Messner recounts the thoughts of a mountaineer during the climb of his life. Messner's compelling chronicle conveys the exhaustion, despair, and exhilaration of mountaineering in the death zone, interwoven with spectacular color photographs.

Paperback book   **$24.95**

Reinhold Messner, Free Spirit
In this revealing autobiography, one of the most innovative and disciplined climbers of our time reflects on his remarkable career. Messner sheds light on the events, motives, and characteristics that have shaped him as an individual and as a climber.

Paperback book   **$19.95**

For more information about these books, contact:

THE MOUNTAINEERS PRESS
outdoor books by the experts

1001 SW Klickitat Way Suite 201 Seattle WA 98134 phone 800.553.4453
www.mountaineersbooks.org

OTHER BOOKS BY EXECUTIVE EXCELLENCE